T0147245

OUR FAITH FLOATS

Two Cwazy Moms' Heartwarming High Seas Adventure

By "The Barefoot Authors":

Debbie Sempsrott & Denise Rogers

Through all of life's ups and downs
We can stay afloat together.

WESTBOW
PRESS
A DIVISION OF THOMAS NELSON
& ZONDERVAN

"Scripture quotations labeled (NIV) are from the Holy Bible, New International Version®, NIV® Copyright © 1973, 1978, 1984, 2011 by Biblica, Inc.® Used by permission. All rights reserved worldwide."

"Scripture quotations marked (NLT) are taken from the Holy Bible, New Living Translation, copyright © 1996, 2004, 2007 by Tyndale House Foundation. Used by permission of Tyndale House Publishers, Inc., Carol Stream, Illinois 60188. All rights reserved."

"Scripture taken from the New King James Version®. Copyright © 1982 by Thomas Nelson, Inc. Used by permission. All rights reserved."

"Scripture taken from The Message. Copyright © 1993, 1994, 1995, 1996, 2000, 2001, 2002. Used by permission of NavPress Publishing Group."

Graphics used with permission by Gretchen Jackson.

Editing by Vicki White.

WestBow Press books may be ordered through booksellers or by contacting:

WestBow Press
A Division of Thomas Nelson & Zondervan
1663 Liberty Drive
Bloomington, IN 47403
www.westbowpress.com
1 (866) 928-1240

Because of the dynamic nature of the Internet, any web addresses or links contained in this book may have changed since publication and may no longer be valid. The views expressed in this work are solely those of the author and do not necessarily reflect the views of the publisher, and the publisher hereby disclaims any responsibility for them.

Any people depicted in stock imagery provided by Thinkstock are models, and such images are being used for illustrative purposes only. Certain stock imagery © Thinkstock.

ISBN: 978-1-4908-3945-5 (sc)
ISBN: 978-1-4908-3946-2 (hc)
ISBN: 978-1-4908-3947-9 (e)

Library of Congress Control Number: 2014910266

Printed in the United States of America.

WestBow Press rev. date: 06/23/2014

Contents

Hope, Hilarity, and Healing for Women

High Seas, High Stress, High Hope ...

Never forget who's in your boat!

"But soon a fierce storm came up.

High waves were breaking into the boat, and it began to fill with water.

Jesus was sleeping at the back of the boat with his head on a cushion.

The disciples woke him up, shouting,

'Teacher, don't you care that we're going to drown?'

When Jesus woke up, he rebuked the wind and said to the waves,

'Silence! Be Still!'

Suddenly the wind stopped, and there was a great calm.

Then He asked them,

'Why are you afraid?

Do you still have no faith?'"

--Mark 4:37-40(NLT)

Isn't it funny how life is a lot like taking a cruise? We all have Cinderella dreams of dressing up for the Captain's night, joining elegantly dressed ladies and gentlemen dining, dancing, and laughing the evening away, all memorialized with formal portraits. Then, at the very first sign of rough seas we are ready to jump ship. Sometimes we are so busy dealing with all of life's struggles that we forget to see the bigger picture. We forget who is in the boat with us. Our faith floats because of a God who stills the storms.

Preface

By Debbie Sempsrott

Balcony room with unobstructed ocean view for two, please. Chocolate Soufflé, sparkling cider, free room service, shows galore, and so much more - this would be romance on the high seas. Our children were partying without us at home, and my husband and I were beyond excited about our long-awaited getaway. We couldn't wait to see the coast of Vancouver, Canada. This would be an adventure, a respite, and a chance for romance.

"The weather started getting rough, the tiny ship was tossed…" You all know the rest of this catchy little tune, so join right in and sing along. The shows were all cancelled. The pools and outside decks were closed. Little bags were taped along the walls for - well, you know what for. All guests were asked not to walk around with drinks because they needed free hands just to stay upright. Even though my husband and I didn't have the cruise we hoped for, we did have a weekend to remember and our relationship was blessed. Sometimes rough waters can cause us to grow more than smooth ones.

My co-author and best friend, Denise, loves to cruise more than any living soul I have ever met. She is the only person I have ever known who actually sailed through a hurricane without realizing it until they went *back* through the storm on their way home. She was having so much fun enjoying her family that a little rough weather didn't even faze her. Because she loves cruising so much, we have taken a couple of cruises together: one with about thirty ladies in a card group, and another for a women's retreat. She also talked me into taking my family on an Alaskan cruise. What I saw of it was amazingly beautiful and breathtaking. I have no words to describe the days I was locked in quarantine with my very own hazmat man, but that is a story for another day.

This book is about the ups-and-downs of life. We are sharing our lives with you: infertility, childbirth, adoption, the terrible twos and beyond, waiting on God, special needs, and other fears we have faced, along with some of our favorite cruise memories, and lots of tears and laughter.

Isn't it funny how life is a lot like taking a cruise? We all have Cinderella dreams of dressing up for the Captain's night, joining elegantly dressed ladies and gentlemen dining, dancing, and laughing the evening away, all captured in formal portraits. Then, at the very first sign of rough seas we're ready to jump ship.

Sometimes we're so busy dealing with life's struggles we forget to see the bigger picture. We forget who is in the boat with us. Our faith floats because of a God who stills the storms. Through all of life's ups and downs, we can stay afloat together.

This book offers, hope, hilarity, and healing. Let's cruise!

Special Thanks

When God's hand is in a project, amazing things begin to happen. Only God can connect the dots that are invisible to us. Twenty plus years ago I (Debbie) lived in Tucson, Arizona where I met a young woman named Vicki. We served together, prayed together, and became best friends. Eventually, Vicki and I both moved to different states, and she got remarried and changed her last name. We lost track of each other at that point. I looked for her on the internet but I didn't know her last name, what city she lived in, or how to find her. About twenty years later we reconnected. How we found each other again was only God's timing and of God's doing. Not only did we pick up our friendship again, but I found out Vicki's passion is editing.

God, in His sovereign timing, reconnected us during the year Denise and I were writing this book. I am so privileged to write a book that involves two of my forever friends. Thank you, Vicki, for coming alongside us and making everything flow together with seamless ease. Your editing is much like your friendship; everything is better when your prayerful loving spirit comes alongside. Our thanks to you is bigger than your big ol' home state of Texas.

All of the sketches and logo for this book were created especially for us by Gretchen Jackson. She has been a Godsend to us! I can't tell you how excited we have been since she joined us in this endeavor. We anxiously await each of her drawings. She has a way of capturing the fun, and makes us look thinner too! So, of course we just love her. They say a picture paints a thousand words and we thank you, Gretchen, for sharing your amazing gift with us!

Last, but certainly not least, we give thanks for our families. They are the stars of this book. Whether we are telling funny stories about them or giving thanks for what God has done in and through our lives, we want to express our love and thanks to them. You will hear about them soon, and for that we sincerely appreciate their forgiveness and patience.

This book is filled with stories about our husbands, children, and the many seasons of our lives. Our families are our greatest gifts. As we have written many of the stories in this book we have been reminded that our most precious memories were often difficult at the time, but in retrospect, they are hilarious. Whether silly or serious, we've recognized God's hand providing and bringing good out of every situation.

We're thankful for friends who have encouraged us through all of the seasons of life that we have shared with you through the stories in this book. Our lives have been greatly blessed because of our church family and friends who have supported us on this journey.

We also want to express our thanks to all of you who are reading this book and pray that you will be blessed. We hope you laugh a bit, cry a bit, and maybe even learn a bit. We pray this book brings a smile to your face and that, by the time you finish reading each story, you find yourself saying, "Aw, I get it." We want to thank you, in advance, for sharing this book with someone else that is in need of a little TLC for their soul.

Most of all, we give thanks and praise to God who has blessed us with everything we need in this life and hope for all eternity.

He has given us the humor, passion, and faith to believe that He is bigger than any obstacles we face.

We thank God for hope, hilarity and healing, even in the midst of high seas and high stress. When Jesus is in our boat there is always a reason for High Hope.

Dedications

One of the most memorable moments on any cruise is the Bon Voyage Celebration. Everyone has big plates of food and they're drinking fruity drinks in fancy glasses. You can smell the burgers grilling and the celebration band is playing songs like "Don't worry, be happy!" Anticipation fills the air.

The send-off message is simply this: *We are not here to just get through another week. We are here to celebrate life! If it rains, we will get out and dance in it. If there are high winds, we will grab a hand and hold on for dear life while enjoying the celebration around us. Our cruise has a limited time-frame. Every moment is precious. We are going to live, love, and laugh. We dare not wait for tomorrow to live well.*

This book is about having joy in all situations. It is about finding the healing medicine of laughter even in tough times. The question is, how can we laugh and live life free of worry and gloom when our cruise is not going the way we want it to go?

We dedicate this book to a dear friend who has been part of this writing adventure. No, she did not write or edit this book, but that would have been much easier for her. Instead, she lives the message of this book. She has experienced the high seas, high stress, and high winds of adversity, but is choosing daily to never forget who is in her boat. We have handed many of our stories to our dear friend even as we wrote them.

I would say to her, "Tell me if this story makes you laugh, cry, and encourages you in some way." Then I would catch myself and say, "Never mind about the crying part, you've already had enough of that."

Our dear friend, Wendy, is recuperating from a long, painful season of chemotherapy. Every day she wants to get off of that cruise and I don't blame her. It's a long, rough ride. You see, Wendy's had a tough time not just because of the cancer. She is the mother of four children, with two youngsters still living at home. While going through cancer with mounting medical bills, she has young children depending on her. Her youngest son is too young to comprehend what she's going through. He is active and wants his mom's constant attention. Being a mom can be challenging on our best days, but it seems more like climbing Mount Everest on our weak, worn-out days.

With each story, Wendy has had the kindness and grace to encourage us to keep writing our new style of inspirational humor to lift the spirits of others who need a diversion from what they are going through. It is because of friends like Wendy that we have a passion and a burden to share our books with dear women who are struggling, sick, having treatment for cancer, or are just in need of some relief through hope, hilarity, and healing.

Dear Wendy, we dedicate this book to you. Thank you for your example, love, and encouragement. You have been an important person to us in this journey. We wish you a long life filled with love, laughter, and strength for the journey.

This book is dedicated to Wendy Brinkman, an amazing mom, friend, encourager, and breast cancer survivor.

"The Beautiful Brinkman's"

Many of us have friends, sisters, moms, and
loved ones who are fighting this struggle.
We may not know your name, but we
wrote this with you in mind.
And so we also dedicate this to you, dear sisters.

Meet the Crew

"A cheerful disposition is good medicine for your health;
Gloom and doom leave you bone tired."—Prov. 17: 22 (The Message)

Debbie Sempsrott & Denise Rogers

Bon voyage … set sail … full speed ahead! Thank you for joining us for this nautical journey through the challenges of a woman's life. We are pleased to assist you on this little cruise. Every "Love Boat" needs a cruise director like Debbie, and every cruise needs a comedian like Denise. Together, we are the Lucy and Ethel of the High Seas.

High Seas, High Stress, High Hope

Funny Denise…

Hello? Yes I would like to book a cruise. Where would I like to go? Some place fun and stress-free. How long would I like to cruise? After the week I've had, sometime between seven days and four months. When do I want to leave? Right now would be perfect!"

That, my dear sisters, is what my dream life is all about. I love to cruise! I can't really put my finger on exactly what it is about walking aboard a cruise ship that makes me take a deep breath and sigh, "*Ah…!*" but I crave that feeling about once a year.

I've cruised to Alaska, Jamaica, Cozumel, the Bahamas, Enseňada, Key West and the Grand Cayman Islands, just to name a few. I've taken groups of women on weekend cruises to Mexico several times. I don't even have to get off the boat. I just need to get on the boat and stay there. My cell phone doesn't receive service, so my clients can't find me. By the time I've had the chocolate melting cake and yelled "Bingo!" a few times, I feel like a brand new person.

Unbelievable as it may seem, I am deathly afraid of water, yet I just love to cruise!

Meet "Funny Denise", the cruise queen comedian.

Debbie Sempsrott

That little phone call, dear friends, is a glimpse of my co-author and partner in chaos, Denise. She's the cruise queen comedian! She loves every minute of cruising, including the planning, even though she truly does hate water!

Denise is an *anomaly,* defined as: 1) A deviation or departure from the normal or common order, form, or rule. 2) One that is peculiar, irregular, abnormal, or difficult to classify.

That explains Denise in a nutshell.

Denise never meets a stranger. She is "Southern friendly" and a cruise ship comedian at heart. I've heard many comedians while cruising and she could give each of them a run for their money. She doesn't have a blonde root in her head. They are Lucille Ball red, as are her facial expressions.

I finally figured out that Denise's humor is a lot like Denise's love for cruising. It soothes her soul, refocuses her mind, and refreshes her spirit. Her wild and wacky humor is like a mini-vacation. I don't have to book a cruise on my bad days. Just a phone call, text, lunch, or any other encounter with Denise leaves me smiling and chuckling. My kids recognize the look on my face and say, "Ah…it's Denise."

Soon you will know exactly what I mean. I just want to warn you in advance that reading her stories in public places may be a big mistake if you are prone to laugh, snort, or do other embarrassing things out loud.

Perhaps you also need to pick up the phone and say, "Hello. Yes, I need a cruise; send me anywhere with no return date." If so, then this is the book for you. Spending a little time with "The Cruise Queen" will be a trip, alright. She has an amazing gift of making people feel comfortable, accepted, and loved through her hugs and the gift of laughter.

As you read Denise's funny experiences, you'll see what I'm talking about. She talks openly about the things most of us would rather hide and forget. She'll make you laugh until you cry. You may even think to yourself, *I can relate, and maybe it's OK to be just who I am - bodily functions, mishaps, and all.* Whether she is talking or writing, it is LOL funny!

It is my privilege and great joy to write with my dear friend, the Cruise Queen Comedian. You will find her in each story as "Funny Denise."

Just Debbie...

I am best known as "Cruise Director Julie." It's my privilege to help you on your journey as life can be a lot like a cruise. For years you dream of that picture-perfect moment. Then the big day comes; you pack your bags and sail off into the sunset. Sometimes we miss the celebration and focus too much on the details. We want the "Suite Life" but we find ourselves stuck in a tiny cubicle - or a prison of our own making.

When you arrive, your first thought may be, "Wow, this room is smaller than my walk-in closet." Then you begin searching for two things, "Where can I put my luggage? And how can I fit in the bathroom?" The answers to these questions quickly become evident. There is nowhere to put a pile of luggage, and bathroom access is inversely proportional to how many people are staying in your miniscule stateroom.

If your family of four is in a tiny, inside room with two bunk beds up and two small beds below, I suggest you hold your luggage while you sleep. Better yet, take a duffle bag so it can double as a pillow. We put our suitcases in the shower, but it is important to remember that your luggage is in there before you turn on the water. Good luck with that, and next time you will definitely want to upgrade to a larger suite.

Speaking of the bathroom in your compact cabin, one size does fit all; it is like one-stop shopping. You can brush your teeth, use the facilities, and/or shower, all at the same time because it is all within reach.

The most interesting thing in the bathroom is the flushing device on the toilets. I'm pretty sure they were made by the people who invented jet engines. When they take off, they really take off! They can - and will - remove any piece of loose clothing that you may have on, and more. If you make the mistake of sitting when you flush, you will no longer need laxatives or headache medicine - it will all be sucked right out of you. In fact, I had a little fluid in my inner ears when I arrived that miraculously disappeared after using our high seas turbo-toilet.

We were invited to enjoy the services of the onboard spa, but with "suction reduction" there was no need for their colon cleansing, bowel irrigation, or colonic hydrotherapy services. This is a free perk that comes with even the most basic room thanks to the "turbo-toilet." It is a force to be reckoned with. Not only will you feel as light as a feather after just one flush, but you will have a new appreciation for being liberated.

It's almost time to roam the ship and see the sights. Your excitement builds - or perhaps it's just another wave of euphoria from your encounter with the High Seas throne? In any case, you realize you can't stay in this position much longer so you start to pry yourself off your suction seat.

As you do, the loud speaker announces, "All passengers must now report to their assigned life boat stations. We know your name and we know what you're doing." (Uh-oh!)

They're calling you for the mandatory life boat drill. The steward does, indeed, have a key to your room and he knows how to use it. They knock on every door to make sure everyone attends. You know you can't stay in your present situation; you must venture out.

If you thought the bathroom adventure was scary, just wait until they describe how many other bottoms are going to fit next to yours in those little grey life boats. By the time they finish the ordeal you're thinking about finding some Dramamine and heading back to your cubicle for a nice long nap.

If you're directionally challenged (or is that just me?) and have problems finding your way around, you will find that cruise ships are huge! They're like floating cities. You can find places in the aft that never connect with the stern and you can literally spend days in the front without ever finding your way to the back. But the smell of food will always lead you to the middle of the ship.

Welcome Aboard! This, my friends, is your dream vacation. You have waited a lifetime to get here. Your credit card bills will be overflowing with remembrances of this dream becoming a reality. If you are the kind of person who does not like crowds, wants to be in control, and enjoys camping out at home, it's too late for you.

Bon voyage … all aboard! You are now setting sail, ready or not. You have a choice to make: you can sit in your little prison cell - I mean stateroom - being rocked by the mighty waves, or you can get up and take part in all of the adventures that are available to you.

Have you ever realized how much life is like a cruise? We have a romantic view of how it will be; we've looked at the brochures and longed for picture-perfect moments. We can't wait to join the club of elegantly put-together, carefree travelers. Our bags are packed and we're ready to go. This is our long-awaited dream.

Then you get there and can't even find a place to unpack your bags. The water is surging and you start feeling unsteady and unsure. You don't know the aft from the stern, or up from down. Just as you begin to have doubts about the journey, you have an encounter that sucks the life out of you. Sometimes life feels like a big old swirling toilet bowl. It seems you keep going around and around and then - flush! - you start wondering, "Where is all the glamour?" Perhaps you got on the wrong cruise, altogether?

Soon, they call your name over the loud speaker for the emergency drill, and for the very first time you think, "I'm going down! Me … in a life boat?" You desperately begin searching for lifelines and one single soul you might know.

Meet "Just Debbie"
(She is more than a pastor's wife!)

Denise Rogers

That, my dear friends, was just a taste of the real Debbie that I have come to know and love. Many people only see her as "the pastor's wife" but to me, she is "just Debbie." She is funny, quirky, and down-to-earth; and she is my friend.

Debbie's nickname has been "Julie" since the day the "Love Boat" first aired on television. Somehow this girl can make you laugh at a story about a turbo-toilet and then apply it to your life in some practical way. Don't ask me how she does it. I try to stump her by giving her crazy, funny stories, but she just starts writing away. This little game we play helps us preserve our sanity.

As you can see from her story about the turbo toilet, Debbie has a zany sense of humor very much like mine. She just doesn't always display hers as openly as I do. Only people who are close to her know that side of her.

Debbie not only has a sense of humor, but she has a way of getting herself into situations that makes us all laugh. She's not only numerically challenged, but directionally challenged, as well. We can - and someday probably will - write an entire book based solely on all of the stories about her being lost. Reading Debbie's escapades will entertain you, and after you see the trouble she gets herself into, you will probably feel a lot better about yourself.

Many people have pointed out that Debbie and I are a lot like Lucy and Ethel. While it is true I have red hair and Lucy's antics, it is Debbie who takes us on so many unforgettable adventures. Like Julie on the "Love Boat" Debbie has a way of helping people see the big picture and getting them involved in great adventures. She not only loves to laugh and have fun but she has a way of seeing

God at work in good times and bad. She can use an ordinary moment to help us see God's presence in our lives.

I love to write about the crazy, ridiculous moments that happen in our lives, but it is Debbie who adds the pop to the stories. She finds something to laugh about, then takes the story and ties it up with a big old bow. She describes those funny moments and adds an "Aw…" factor. You know, the moment when you say, "Aw, now I get it, and I see a glimpse of God at work in my life."

She makes me laugh and I think you will, too. Many introduce her as a pastor's wife or for her position in ministry, but she would be the first to tell you that she prefers to be known as a real, ordinary person. As she would tell you, she is "just Debbie."

We hope that our unique perspectives, different personalities, and various gifts will make you laugh, look inward and upward; as that is what this friendship has done for us. Join us on this cruise down Memory Lane as we reveal our struggles and laugh through the tears. Maybe what we have learned will help you deal with your own rough seas.

We have high hopes to share with you as we cruise together.

Choose the Cruise

*"Choose this day whom you will serve … but as for
me and my house we will serve the Lord."*
—Joshua 24: 15b (paraphrased)

Just Debbie

Funny Denise

"The send-off message is simply this: We are not here to
just get through another week. We are here to celebrate
life! If it rains, we will get out and dance in it. If there are
high winds, we will join hands and hold on for dear life
while enjoying the celebration going on around us. Our
cruise has a limited time-frame. Every moment is precious.
We choose to live, love, and laugh."
--Debbie Sempsrott

We dare not miss the cruise!

Funny Denise …

What is it that floats your boat?

I went to a Women of Faith Conference a year ago and heard a speaker ask that question. He said, "It's not what you do for a living, but it is that one thing that soothes your soul."

As I sat in the stands I thought to myself, "What is it that really floats my boat? It can't be accounting; accounting couldn't float a canoe made of Ivory soap! What really soothes my soul is telling stories and making people laugh or smile."

Debbie wanted to write this book to reflect the struggles that we all deal with and give other women encouragement and hope. I wanted to write about all the deranged things that pass through a woman's mind while trying to live through the ups and downs of everyday life. My view of the seasons of a woman's life is very simple. There are diapers, hormones, first bra, tampons, PMS, infertility waiting on God, pregnancy, post-partum, the terrible twos and beyond, puberty, calamity, and moments of total insanity.

Then the day comes when your child is ready to leave the nest and you would give everything you have to live through all of that parenting craziness again. You would give anything you own and all that is within your power just to see that smile and hear that little voice say "Mama" just one more time. Oh, to be able to kiss those little cheeks again!

You know you need to have your head examined because every time you look at that young man with a goatee, you see the face of your little boy. Somehow your entire life has passed before your eyes as quickly as a weekend cruise to Enseñada.

Just Debbie ...

Life is a lot like a cruise. One minute you're looking forward to it; then you blink and find yourself debarking and dreaming of your next cruise. We're a lot like that in our everyday lives. When our kids are little we dream of getting uninterrupted sleep, wondering when our house will ever be clean again and how long it will be until we enjoy some independence. When will we actually have the bathroom to ourselves without someone knock-knock-knocking at the door? And in the blink of an eye, we look up and that precious little boy is heading out for his own cruise. How did that happen?

Suddenly, we realize life passed us by while we were working so hard at living. Life is not just about the destination; it is all about the journey. Most importantly, it's about celebrating the moments in every season of life.

Perhaps you remember the old TV sitcom "The Love Boat" where the passengers go through unexpected twists and turns through the course of their voyage, even though their only intent was to have a little fun? The cruise that God has in mind for us is very similar.

The Bible uses the word "agape" for the journey we are called to live. This is an unconditional kind of love that weeps with those who weep and rejoices with those that rejoice. It desires the best for everyone around us. The cruise that God has selected for us is centered on people, not things. It doesn't require us to make things around us perfect; it's about making us perfect…complete and mature through love.

The question is, what do we choose to do with the cruise God has given us?

Funny Denise …

There's nothing more fun than gathering your best buddies and taking a road trip, or even better, a cruise! My plan one year was to gather a group of women in my church and head out for a weekend cruise. It really didn't matter where we went as long as we were all together. Laughter is the best medicine, no matter what you are going through in your life. Plenty of medical statistics support laughter as a health benefit, but whenever ladies get together telling funny stories and laughing, God is there. He melts down the walls between us.

We gathered a group of twenty-five women and headed out to the open seas for a weekend getaway. I had the privilege of taking my mom on this cruise and we had a suite. It was like the Presidential suite, and it was sweet! To make things even better, we were sharing it with Debbie and her daughter, Chelsea. It was so large we could have shared it with twenty more people, so we invited a group of ladies to join us as we departed.

The booking agent had sent a bottle of sparkling cider to our room and I had ordered a platter of hors d'oeuvres. You know how there are some things in your life that only a husband should do because men are not mechanically challenged? Well, opening a bottle of sparkling cider is one of those things. I'd like to say I'm too young to remember Coke bottles with tops that required a bottle opener, but that would be a lie. This particular bottle needed an opener – at least that's what I assumed. (I have since found out it was probably a screw top.)

As I was searching for a bottle opener, Debbie decided the edge of the counter would work just fine. I'd seen rednecks do that with a beer bottle in a Texas bar, but never by a pastor's wife on a cruise ship. All the ladies were watching.

Recognizing the potential for disaster, I went to the bathroom to get a towel for the floor. I came back and told her this was not going to work. No matter how I looked at it, it was going to spill. The problem is, Debbie's brain translates the words "This will not work" into "This is gonna be great!"

In Texas, just before something bad happens, you frequently hear, "Hey, y'all watch this!" Debbie would have made a great

Texan because this was going to be a Texas moment if there ever was one.

I bent down to lay the towel on the floor, explaining in great scientific detail that, due to basic physics, it was going to make a mess. Debbie placed the bottle top on the edge of the counter and, in true redneck fashion, slammed her other hand down on it.

Glass went everywhere; the top flew off the bottle and hit the glass window, the cider spewed all over my hair, our clothes, her face, my mom's face (who was across the room), the balcony window, the carpet and the ceiling. We were one big sticky mess! My wet hair curled up on one side and the hair that was still dry stayed straight on the other. I couldn't see through my glasses, but I heard the best sound ever - Debbie's uncontrollable laughter!

The mess didn't matter. It didn't matter that there were glass shards everywhere and we had no cider to drink. The most important thing was the unrestrained laughter that reverberated throughout the room filling it with the sweet sounds of shared friendship. The ladies were beyond grins and giggles and so was I.

It's not the "perfect" in life that makes us happy - it's the imperfect mixed with the laughter of friends. It was an over-the-top moment that we will never forget.

Just Debbie ...

When was the last time you laughed so hard you lay on the floor in reckless abandon? Many of us are consumed with day-to-day pressures, worries, and fears. We analyze and micromanage everything around us and have lost the ability to laugh at life's little mishaps.

There is a woman in the Bible who also cracked open a bottle, although it was not sparkling cider, but expensive perfume. She spent the little money she had to purchase this extravagant gift, and then she wasted it all in one continuous pour.

Do you know how many hungry people could have been fed with the money she spent on that one bottle? Mary let it flow right over the feet of her Master, her Savior, and her God. She was totally present, living with abandon in that moment, opening her whole heart to celebrate the presence of the living God in her life. Not everyone understood her gift, but even though they criticized her for it, I bet she was filled with a lot of joy. This was a "Hey, y'all watch this" moment.

The Bible tells us the story of her expensive gift in John 12:7-8 (NLT). That perfume was worth a year's wages. She not only poured it on Jesus' feet, but she washed his feet with her hair.

Judas had his own greedy agenda and found fault with her gift. But Jesus replied, "Leave her alone. She did this in preparation for my burial. You will always have the poor among you, but you will not always have me." (John 12:7 NLT)

The time for Jesus' crucifixion was rapidly approaching and, without even knowing it, Mary's beautiful act of love in anointing Jesus with oil, helped prepare Him - mentally, emotionally and spiritually - for what was to come.

It would be such a shame for us to miss the laughter and joy of cracking open that bottle in celebration. Life is not just about the destination; it's about the journey. It's about the lessons learned, memories made, and celebrations that we cherish along the way.

So far, I've been on five cruises. I have loved every one of them and I can tell you that no two cruises were the same. One time my husband and I went on a repositioning cruise - a one-way cruise to take the ship back to its port to prepare for the new season of travel. We got an excellent rate and had a balcony room. It was fabulous!

We soon found out why this type of cruise was so economical. It seems ships travel in certain directions during certain seasons for good reasons: turbulence, sea sickness and Dramamine!

The waves were hitting the ship so hard the passengers weren't allowed on deck. There were no shows, the pools and hot tubs were closed, and all outside activities were cancelled. I hoped the movie would not be "Titanic." I was a little nervous. (Alright, I can't lie in a faith-based book. I was downright afraid at times!)

I wanted to celebrate and enjoy the view, but I couldn't see the scenery for the huge waves crashing all around us! I started thinking back on the life boat drill they had us do at the outset of the cruise. With trepidation, I wondered about those tiny boats: how would we get to them across decks flooded from the towering waves, and how would they not be full of water?

There is a story much like this found in the gospels. Jesus and the disciples were out on the water in a boat. The storms came up and the disciples were scared to death. Yet, Jesus, the son of God, was right there in the boat. They awakened Him and, with only His words, He calmed the storm.

In modern lingo, he would have said, "Really, fear over faith?" What He meant was basically, where is your faith?

Ladies, this is the simple truth: we do not get to pick the weather for our cruise. We are not in charge of the people around us and we may find ourselves in some pretty tight living situations where we face an experience that just sucks the life out of us. Unfortunately, we can't control any of that. However, as women, we can choose to crack open some bubbly and let it flow - or fly - glass and all. Our choice today is to celebrate with joy whether we are in rough or calm seas.

Getting back to our original question, what floats your boat isn't what you do for a living. It's the passion of your heart that soothes your soul. This passion is your perfume. Are you willing to pour it all out for God?

What's stopping you from taking that dream cruise of a lifetime? There will be inconveniences, challenges, and some waves along the way. But if you look up, you'll see Jesus' smiling face right there in the boat with you. Will you falter in fear, or reach out and celebrate life with true abandon? A little sparkling cider never hurt anyone and the laughter of a sold-out life will surely make God smile.

Celebration is a "Hey, y'all watch this" kind of moment. In spite of the wind, waves, and weather, people always take notice when we choose the cruise!

Don't Miss the Boat

"It was by faith that Noah built a large boat to save his family from the flood. He obeyed God, who warned him about things that had never happened before."—Heb. 11:7 (NLT)

the Ark

Life passed us by while we were working so hard at *living*.
Life is not just about the destination;
it is all about the journey.
Most importantly, it is about celebrating the
moments in every single season of life.

What a shame it would be to miss the boat!

Funny Denise …

"Let's Cruise!" Those two words alone can transport me out of any dull workday, any argument with my spouse, or any boring house cleaning chore. My husband has no idea what I'm talking about when I say cruising is the best vacation ever. I mean, where else can you go that you can have your room cleaned and bed turned down every day, with free 24-hour room service, exotic foods, endless entertainment, and visit the places of your dreams?

Life on a cruise brings out the real me. I totally cut loose and enjoy myself. My mom and I have had some moments on cruise ships that I probably wouldn't experience with anybody else. My mom is a kick; she's an introvert in the truest sense of the word. However, she has the best sense of humor. As goofy as I am, she never judges me; she just lets me be me. But doing that inevitably puts her in some strange circumstances.

For instance, one time we were on a huge cruise ship heading to Cozumel. It was Mom's very first cruise and the ship was overwhelming to her, so I tried never to leave her side. One evening, Mom and I decided to venture out to find food. We had heard the food was on deck 12, so we went to the nearest elevator to head upstairs. We got our plates of food and decided to sit outside and eat while enjoying the ocean breeze. After an hour or so we decided to head back to our room and call it a night. As we were heading back to our room, the ship's night life was just picking up. Mom and I got in an elevator and looked at each other as if to say, "What floor are we on again?" We went from floor to floor and, as the doors opened, we would glance out to see if we recognized anything familiar, step back in and punch another floor. This went on for what seemed like twenty minutes.

Finally, the inevitable happened. Mom and I got the giggles and with that came the ultimate splash down. As tears were running down her face I asked if she had on a Depend. She was laughing so hard she couldn't speak, but shook her head no. I knew I couldn't hold it much longer and was wishing I had worn a Depend, myself. There we stood, floor-after-floor, as people got on and off. The doors opened and shut over and over, but there we stayed, knowing we couldn't get off that elevator until we were alone. We rode the elevator for over an hour just laughing and crying. All the time we were wondering how in the world we could get off the elevator - soaked!

An idea dawned on me, so I leaned in and whispered, "Follow my lead." She looked frightened but agreed. At the next floor we stepped through the crowd on the elevator and I began to have a loud conversation chastising her. Why did she want to go swimming so late at night and not at least bring a towel? We stepped off the elevator and as the door closed I heard roaring laughter, just when I thought we were in the clear!

I have so much fun cruising with my family that one year I completely missed one important little fact: we were sailing through a hurricane! All my friends at home were sending panicked e-mails, but I was merrily sailing away. Hurricane Irene was hitting the Bahamas as we were rerouted around the storm.

We sailed blissfully unaware that several ships had left passengers on islands with no way home due to the emergency warnings. As we sailed through the hurricane on our last night at sea, our beds didn't just rock from side to side, our feet came out of our beds and our heads hit the head rests. I had to admit, in this case, dry land was looking better after all. Cruising is a lot like life; it has its ups and downs.

I persuaded my BFF to cruise to Alaska with her family. I have been on two Alaskan cruises with breathtaking scenery resulting in lifetime memories. Debbie will certainly remember her Alaskan cruise forever, but not so much for the scenery.

She enjoyed the first half of her cruise, sampling all of the exotic foods prepared out on the open seas - at least until she decided to try the calamari. After a few bites she decided not to do that again.

The next morning she was up and outside early, enjoying the fresh air and taking photos of the glaciers when all of a sudden it hit her. She had to locate a bathroom fast! Now, Debbie is directionally challenged in a parking garage so can you imagine her dilemma on a cruise ship. She finally located her room and immediately began a deeply meaningful relationship with the porcelain throne. Her husband was awakened from his melodic snoring to hear some not-so-melodic roaring coming from the bathroom. Those of you who have cruised before will remember how small those bathrooms really are. For those of you unfamiliar with cruise ship bathrooms, try to picture kneeling in a room the size of a matchbox. She thought it was sea sickness or maybe the calamari, but things kept getting worse.

Before she knew it, a little man appeared with a wheelchair to give her a ride to the underbelly of the ship. This is the section of the ship that no one wants to visit … ever. She covered her head with a hoodie so no one could see who was being rolled through the lobby.

Debbie was hoping for a little sea sickness patch to take away what ailed her. Instead, she was told that over a hundred people had been diagnosed with the Norovirus on this particular cruise. She was the next lucky winner, but there was not going to be any chicken dinner! The infirmary gave her some shots where the "sun don't shine" and before she could say, "Yo-ho-ho and a bottle of Pepto," she was in Quarantine.

Being in Quarantine is bad enough, but for Debbie it didn't stop there. Every day she was visited by her very own hazmat man in a white jumpsuit with a mask and gloves like those worn on the Space Station. Periodically, they would deliver her limited foods and clean her room from top to bottom. Some folks really know how to cruise in style!

Just Debbie …

Now that the cat is out of the bag and you know I had my very own Hazmat man you're probably wondering if I'd ever go on another cruise. The answer is *absolutely!* I have since gone on a cruise and had a wonderful time. Alaska provided some of the best - and worst -moments of my life. However, my most memorable cruise was my first.

When you hear the words "dream vacation" what picture comes to mind? For me, the picture that always comes to mind is blue water ... lots of crystal clear water. For as long as I can remember, especially since I got married, I dreamed of going on a cruise. What in the world could be more exciting than sailing out on the ocean with an endless supply of free food, tropical music, swimming pools, and of course, more free food. Just the midnight dessert buffet with all the ice sculptures would be worth the trip!

After fourteen years of marriage, we finally took our long-awaited dream vacation. We were sailing on a Christian cruise to the Bahamas, departing Miami, Florida on a hot and humid July day. The band was playing island tunes like, "Don't worry, be happy!"

Many of our friends were on board and we loved having dinner with them, going to movies, Christian concerts, and shore excursions to wonderful white sand beaches. We loved walking around the deck each evening and enjoying beautiful sunsets.

One night we watched our ship rescue seven Cuban refugees. Everyone cheered as they were pulled to safety. Not only were we excited about this dream vacation of a lifetime, but we had other reasons to celebrate. We had been selected by a birthmother to adopt a little baby boy! After one failed adoption, we were finally ready to walk down that road again. We had high hopes and we were celebrating on the high seas.

Our claustrophobic little room was the size of a matchbox and something weird was going on with me. I was on a boat with all this wonderful free food twenty-four hours a day but I couldn't stand the smell of it. How wrong was that? Our room was located close to the kitchen and I could smell food cooking all day and night. That was not going over very well with me at all. In addition, at lunch time I would be so hungry I would eat two hamburgers *and* a hot dog, but later in the day, when they would serve our wonderful gourmet dinner, all I could think about was going to sleep. It was really strange!

One night, I lay in bed wide awake with a pain in my side, feeling something was wrong - different - and it wouldn't go away. As I lay there, I began to pray and a thought came to my mind, but it wasn't my thought. This strong prompting simply spoke to my heart, "You have wanted to sail the seas all your life and at the first second of fear you want to go home." I would need to remember those words in the days to come - and remember them, I would!

Do you recall the Bible story when the disciples went on a three hour cruise? I can't help but sing that catchy little tune from the old TV show. "The weather started getting rough. The tiny ship was tossed. If not for the courage of the fearless crew the Minnow would be lost."

Matthew 8 tells us the story of the disciples' cruise with Jesus. I, for one, would love to know the name of their tiny little ship. Perhaps it was called "The Master's Minnow". Anyway, the winds were getting rough and the tiny ship was tossed. Jesus was asleep in the back of the boat, and the disciples were not exactly a fearless crew. "The disciples went and woke him, saying 'Lord, save us! We're going to drown'! He replied, 'You of little faith, why are you so afraid'? Then he got up and rebuked the winds and the waves, and it was completely calm." They asked, "What kind of man is this? Even the winds and the waves obey Him!" (Mt. 8:25-27 NIV)

It has been said that we can fear God, or everything else. When God, Himself, is in the boat, life takes on a new perspective. Matthew 14 tells the story of the disciples taking another short cruise, only this time Jesus was not in the boat. It was around four in the morning and Jesus had sent them ahead to cross to the other side, while he went up the mountainside alone to pray. The boat was being battered by the winds and waves, and they were all alone. The disciples looked up to see a figure walking toward them on the water. If you thought they were scared before, you can imagine how they felt seeing a ghost!

Jesus spoke to them and said, "Take courage. It is I. Don't be afraid." (Matthew 14:27 NIV) You have got to love the apostle Peter in this story because this guy is the Comeback Kid. He rebounds so quickly with faith that he asks Jesus if he can come and join Him for a late night stroll on the water. (Actually it was more like an early morning dip.) Peter was doing alright until he saw the winds and waves; as his fears rose, he began to sink. He cried out to Jesus to save him. Jesus immediately reached out His hand and caught Peter.

His simple question to Peter was, "You of little faith, why did you doubt?" (Matthew 14:31 NIV)

These stories are the message that God brought to my mind as I lay in bed that fearful, sleepless night. God was asking me the very same question, "Do you trust me?" Not only did I need to answer that question that night, but in the days ahead I would need to decide if I would stay safely on land or "walk on the water" with God.

Have you ever noticed that the greatest miracles in the Bible usually come right after a big storm, high winds, dark times, or fearful encounters? It is at precisely those moments when we see

God-sized interventions in our lives. We may even call them miracles. God stills the sea, heals the sick, raises the dead, and, yes, walks on the water.

If you knew a hurricane was heading your way but you would see God's very hand and presence in the midst of the storm, would you climb in the boat? Many people would just stay safely on shore and wait to hear other's testimonies. Would you be the person who had enough faith to ask the bold question of Jesus, "Lord, can I walk with you?"

Late that night I heard all of these questions in my mind and I answered them in my heart. I would choose to fear God versus being afraid of everything else. I have always wanted to see God work in my life, so I decided to ride it out with God. As you may have guessed, after fourteen years of marriage, I was pregnant just as we were about to adopt a baby.

Shortly after the cruise, my husband and I went to his favorite manly mall. They have jumbo this and jumbo that - everything a man loves in a shopping place. As we walked through the front door, I saw a double stroller. Without thinking, I said, "I think we're going to need that!" There's nothing like buying in bulk, right?

I'm eternally thankful that I didn't miss the boat because of my fears - and, oh yes, you guessed it - I would shortly be walking on water holding two babies.

"And when they climbed into the boat, the wind died down. Then those who were in the boat worshiped him, saying, 'Truly you are the Son of God'." --Mt. 14:32-33 (NIV)

Chelsea (left) & Chad (right)
(They are just 6 ½ months apart!)
(And YES, this is the famous stroller that I
saw in the jumbo-this and that store.)

It would be Double the Blessing, Double the Joy!

The Mommy Club

"For you created my inmost being; you knit
me together in my mother's womb."
—Ps. 139: 13 (NIV)

I think infertility is the most silent
medical problem of our day.
No one talks about it.
People don't die from it, but it certainly crushes hearts.
--Debbie Sempsrott

"Let it be to me as You have said."

—Mary's prayer

Just Debbie …

Have you ever wanted to be in a club that seemed inaccessible to you? The people in it all looked like they were having so much fun; they shared interests and activities, and butterfly filled blue skies just seemed to constantly surround them. At least, that is how it always looks from the outside. I remember those days so well.

The club I wanted to join more than any other was "The Mommy Club". Their lives were filled with baby showers, cute little clothes, family portraits, Mother's Day celebrations, and all of the joy that came with hearing sweet little voices saying the word, "Mommy." What made it harder was seeing in my husband's eyes that he was just dying to get out that little bat and ball and play in the yard with his little boy.

One of the things Denise and I share as friends is that both of us waited a long, long time to join the Mommy Club. They call this journey "infertility". To any new friends reading this story who find themselves in these particular rough waters, we hope our story makes you smile a bit. We can both see God's healing hand as we look back on this season of our lives.

Funny Denise ...

I got married at the age of twenty-two to the only man I ever dated. I met him in college and immediately knew he was the man for me. He was tall, muscular, auburn hair, athletic and just plain handsome, but that was not what attracted me to him. He was a gentleman; polite and honest in the truest form. He actually dated me for awhile before even asking permission to kiss me. In the past thirty-something years, I have yet to open a door or pull out my own chair. He's the definition of a west Texas cowboy.

After graduation, we married and decided to wait to have a family. We both wanted careers and a home. The bottom line was that we wanted to enjoy life as a couple before raising a family. After a year of watching our friends have children, we decided that our fun needed to start with a family and not before. Thus began the hardest time in our marriage.

Once I decided I wanted children, I wanted them now! We tried for years with absolutely no success. Was there something wrong with us? I went to the doctor and he said to just stop trying so hard.

"Don't think about it all the time. Just let it happen, 'cause it will."

Where in the world did these doctors study? Did they really get a degree in medicine?

We began to get suggestions on how to get pregnant from people at our church. This is the weirdest conversation you can have with an elderly lady at your church. One of the ladies went on to tell me that she had a hard time having a baby boy so she told her husband to stand on his head for thirty minutes. Another woman told me that she had a hard time getting pregnant, so she came up with a concoction that involved applying bags of ice in areas that should never *ever* be frozen. This was all just TMI (too-much-info) to hear at church from my grey-haired friends while singing "Blest Be the Tie That Binds"!

After seven years of trying everything known to man (and grey haired women), I tried praying. One month later, I was pregnant. The first three months I gained one pound. The doctor was concerned and said I needed to eat more. On my fourth month I had gained 16 pounds. The doctor said, "Stop eating!" The fifth month I gained 18 pounds. The doctor said, "Enough!" The sixth month I went in to weigh and stripped naked in front of the nurses, doctors, and God Himself. I still gained 18 more pounds. The doctor just shook his head and said "What are you eating?"

What was I eating? Well, it might be easier to say what I was *not* eating. Anything that grows in the yard was out, everything else was in. I found myself craving Subway sandwiches, foot long chili dogs, and mini sausages. In Texas they call these Beer sausages as they are fermented in vinegar. These little sausages come in a big jar. I made it through the first jar with my tongue still intact. However, about midway through the second jar I could feel my tongue begin to swell - similar to Pinocchio's nose.

You could say I overdid it just a tad. To this day, my son will not eat anything with vinegar.

My husband told me I needed to exercise. We lived exactly half a mile from a Subway sandwich shop. He told me if I walked the half mile to the Subway shop instead of driving, I could reward myself with a six inch sub when I got home. What he didn't know was that I ate a foot long while I was sitting there regaining the strength to plod back home, and I had my little six inch sub as a reward after I plopped myself back in my blue recliner.

Not only did I love Subway, but there was a Sonic between my house and my office. So, every other day I would order two, foot-long chili dogs and a large order of chili-cheese Tater Tots, and dip them in ranch dressing. Perhaps you have heard of the American Heart Association's four food groups. I had my very own Food Pyramid ... Fried, Fats, and Floating in Sauce. (Sad, but true - 50 pounds worth of truth!)

Bless his heart, my helpful doctor told me I needed to eat "green things" like salad. As I mentioned before, I do not like to work in the yard, nor do I like to *eat* the yard. My husband decided he would get me to eat spinach as it was supposed to be good for me. Maybe he just watched too much "Popeye" while he was growing up. Nevertheless, this was his plan and there was no stopping him on his quest to bring the great outdoors inside. While I don't like salad, I do like sauces, dressings, and anything that "helps the medicine go down."

It was the holiday season and I was thinking, "Christmas cookies!" My husband was thinking in terms of Christmas, too. There was definitely a lot of green and red on his mind. He would take a big handful of spinach and tomatoes and plop them on my plate. I would make a holiday toast and drink the Caesar dressing. Did that count?

Why would a doctor even think to ask me what I was eating? Was he not from Texas? Being from the panhandle state I was handling and eating everything in the pan! Shoot, I was eating for the entire state! Had he not heard that everything is bigger and better in Texas - including my appetite?

As you have probably guessed by now, I toasted the New Year with my Caesar dressing as we anxiously awaited our new arrival. My son was due the first of February. After forty weeks had passed, the doctor said, "I am sure it will be any day now." After forty-one weeks and no Braxton Hicks, the baby was not dropping and I began to wonder if he thought of me as the local Residence Inn.

The day before my forty-second week, the doctor decided to induce labor and see what would happen. I went to the hospital on a Thursday and they came in to get me prepped. Yeah, that was the word they used - *prepped*.

A nurse came in with a pail of warm water and a hose. I naïvely obeyed as she told me to roll over and take a deep breath. All I could think was, "This is just not right!" Followed shortly by my second thought, "All I have to do is make it to the bathroom and it will be OK."

Once the nurse was finished with her little chore, I took my 200 pound body and duck-walked to the bathroom. Thus began the weirdest hour of my life up to that point. Noises arose from my body that even frightened my husband. He said, "Just get this over with." I tried but it was a slow, drawn-out process.

After an hour, I got up and went back to lie on the bed. The nurse put a plastic bed pan under me and my husband said, "She'll crush that. You need a metal one." The nurse laughed and within ten minutes I had crushed the bed pan. She brought in another plastic bed pan and, again, I crushed it. The third bed pan was metal and fresh from the freezer.

Ten hours after being induced, I was wheeled into the operating room for a C-section. Twenty-eight minutes later I was looking at my gift from God ... a healthy 10 pound baby boy!

It was Sunday when the nurse came in and said, "Hun, you are going to have to go to the bathroom before you go home." There was only one difficulty; my system was obviously shut down for the remainder of my stay. I wanted so badly to go home, but all systems were a no go.

Like most husbands, my husband is a fixer and a true Texas gentleman. So, he just decided to "git `er done" himself! No lovelier offering was ever given on my behalf. The nurse was so proud! I took my little bundle of boy joy and we headed home as a family for the first time.

Just Debbie ...

I am so glad Denise can make me laugh about the journey, and I am so thankful for the place where I find myself today. But

I have a few memories that have changed how I look at the long, winding road of infertility. I can empathize with my fellow sisters who are still wishing, waiting, and wondering.

I think infertility is the most silent medical problem of our day. No one talks about it. People don't die from it, but it certainly crushes hearts.

One of the worst memories I have about infertility actually happened at church. It was Mother's Day - the day on which my heart bore an extra-heavy burden because I had still not joined that elusive Mommy Club - and I was preparing to lead worship for the morning service. I had put together a special PowerPoint presentation with a song to play as the church gave away roses to honor all the mothers in the congregation. One of the ladies walked up to me saying, "Happy Mother's Day" and handed me a rose. I stood there with an awkward look on my face and she quickly realized what she had just done. I'm sure she didn't quite know how to get out of this uncomfortable situation, so she reached out and tore the rose off, leaving me with the stem. She made a little joke about how I only got the stem but not the rose. I'm sure she felt bad, but I left the room quickly for the little girls' room. I really didn't want her, or anyone else to see how bad that hurt.

My husband and I were married 14 years without children. All our friends had kids. My much younger sister had a child. Even the people who came to live with us briefly got pregnant while staying in our home. The journey seemed so long and unfair.

The Bible says children are a gift from God, so I wondered why everyone else was opening all the presents. In the long years ahead, we went through a multitude of tests, procedures and even a surgery to correct things.

The comfort God gave me during those days has given me a compassion that I feel compelled to pass on to many other young women I have come to love and care for. One of my young friends has had to face more than one miscarriage. While she walked silently through those dark times she would look around and see all of her friends having their babies. She not only had to deal with that, but she rubbed shoulders with other young women who were pregnant and unhappy. Would they even keep their baby or be able to provide for them?

God reminded me during those years of wondering, watching, and waiting that He is ultimately in charge of all of our days. He doesn't cause harm or sin. God is always good, but the scriptures definitely tell us that only God can open the womb. Only God creates life.

Abraham and Sarah are amazing examples of a couple that were blessed by God more than any of us can imagine, but they just didn't know it … yet! Sarah got tired of waiting on God and came up with her own plan. She found a handmaiden for her husband - not a smooth move. The world is still paying today for that single act of rebellion. In the midst of this, God promised Abraham that his descendants would be like the stars in the sky. Now that kind of promise should count for something, shouldn't it?

Genesis 18 tells the story of Abraham and Sarah's encounter with God. When Sarah was told of God's promise to give them a son, she laughed. She was old … really old!

The Bible tells us that God asked Abraham, "Why did Sarah laugh?" In Genesis 18:14a (NIV) He asks, "Is there anything too hard for the Lord?"

That is the question we all need to answer in our heart of hearts. Is there anything too hard for God? Can God use us in any way He chooses? Can He choose our path and our course in life? Can He choose whether He gives us an Isaac or perhaps a Samuel, like Hannah received after her long wait?

I can relate to Sarah's reactions. I begged, pleaded, planned, was angry at God, and sometimes others. One night when I couldn't sleep, I got out of bed, sat down at my piano and started to play a song for God. I called the song, "I belong to You." God and I were having a conversation. Finally, it became a two-way conversation. I was listening and responding with submission. I had my plans and my dreams, but I decided to lay them all in His lap. I would walk the road that He had picked out for me and I would choose to walk it in faith that the God who loved me would provide for me. I told God, "From now on, we will do this Your way."

That night I began praying differently. Many of us want to be in control of our lives. We want to decide how many children we have and what month they will be born. The only problem is that God is God, and we are not. I stopped trying to figure everything out and stopped all of the endless processes that were leading nowhere. Instead, I told God that I wanted children and I understood He already knew this. I would be a foster parent, run a home for kids, adopt, or whatever He had in mind. I would continue teaching in a Christian school and love the kids He brought my way. It was His call, not mine.

I love the story in the Bible that tells us of God's encounter with Mary. The angel said to Mary, "Greetings, you who are highly favored! The Lord is with you." (Luke 1:28 NIV) Mary was afraid and feeling the weight of her circumstances, so God sent an angel to tell her how much He loved her and that she was favored in His eyes. The angel goes on to tell her about God's plan for her baby and not to be afraid. I bet she needed to hear those words. My favorite words are when He reminds her that HE is with her.

We all get afraid; we just do. Only God can step into fear and bring peace. She was favored and she was not supposed to live in fear. God was getting ready to use her in a mighty way. The only step remaining was her response to God's invitation. We must admit that her circumstances were quite unusual, to say the least. It has only happened one time in the history of humanity. How in the world was she going to explain any of this to anybody – her mom, her dad, her community, and oh yes, Joseph?

So, here comes the big moment for Mary's response. What questions will she ask? What demands of God will she make? Here it is … wait for it! She simply says, "Let it be to me as you have said." That's it. A modern short summary of her words in the first chapter of Luke, goes something like this, "I am the servant, you are my God, and we are doing this Your way."

Mary's prayer says it all. She begins with these words, "I am the Lord's servant," and then she submits everything to a God who is greater and higher. I think Mary's prayer still says it all for any of us who are seeking to be in the Mommy Club.

"I am the Lord's servant. May everything you have said about me come true." --Luke 1:38 (NLT)

Those Terrible Two's

"Keep me as the apple of your eye;
Hide me in the shadow of your wings."
—Psalms 17:8(NIV)

Denise & Bill

When God sits on His porch with His children, I wonder what He sees in us. Does He use the word "pistol" to describe you or me? Does He say, "I'm not finished with my story yet; there is more …" Does He go on to tell of strewn boxes and messes that have accumulated from our rebellious actions and attitudes? This, I have to ponder. Have you ever wondered how God feels about you when you have a really bad, horrible, no good, temper tantrum kind of day?

"Yes, baby, you are perfect in my eyes!"

Funny Denise ...

Ever prayed for something for so long that you started to believe it would never happen, and then it did but you didn't realize your prayers were answered? It was June 1991, and I was packing for a family vacation to camp on the beach at Corpus Christi, Texas. My folks, my brother and his wife, and my husband and I were heading to the coast for a much needed week of deep sea fishing, swimming, lying out in the sun, and plenty of family games. I just couldn't wait to get there.

I needed something to take my mind off the fact that I had been trying to get pregnant for almost seven years and felt I was wandering in the desert with no answer from God. I was afraid to think that maybe His answer was no.

We were all having a marvelous family vacation and toward the end of the week we decided to go deep sea fishing. I was told to take Dramamine at least two hours before leaving, and take it again every 3 hours while on the boat. I caught two fish, but for the life of me I don't remember a thing about that boat trip. What I do remember is not being sick while those around me were not as lucky.

The week went by way too fast and soon my husband and I were headed west, back to Abilene, while the rest of my family headed home to south Texas. You need to understand that I am a fried food connoisseur and have never met a French fry I didn't love. We had just reached Austin when I told my husband I was feeling sick and thought I needed some food. We stopped at the closest greasy spoon we could find and took a table close to the window. I ordered a bacon double cheeseburger, extra mayo and ketchup, the largest order of fries – extra grease – and a large sweet tea. All southern women must have their sweet tea!

I excused myself, went to the restroom, and couldn't get past that gnawing feeling in my stomach. I returned to the table to see the food had arrived and I began to eat a French fry. The minute I tried to swallow I was nauseated. I told my husband I must have the flu. We boxed up the food and headed back to Abilene. Within ten minutes of leaving the restaurant I had tossed the food out the window. The smell was unbearable.

Five hours later, we arrived home and I was in pretty bad shape. I took to my bed and didn't want to move. By late evening my husband was worried and questioning whether he needed to get me some medication. I didn't get this sick very often. I said no to the medicine, thinking I just needed to sleep. At 10:00 p.m. it was like a light bulb went on over his head. He sat straight up in bed and said, "I think I know why you might be sick."

I said, "Do you think I'm … pregnant?"

He said, "I will be right back." He took off for the store and arrived home 10 minutes later with the pregnancy test. The next five minutes seemed to take an eternity as we waited on the results. Sure enough, I was pregnant!

I had prayed for this day for over seven years and when it finally happened it was the last thing to cross my mind. Why is it when God answers our prayers we are so often shocked?

In February 1992, we welcomed our ten pound bundle of joy into our lives and our hearts. I just knew he was the most handsome, adorable, intelligent child ever put on this earth! My son, Bill, could do no wrong – at least he could do no wrong in my eyes, until about 18 months later.

Bill started his terrible twos six months early. It didn't matter what I told him not to do, he had to do it. Until he was old enough to go to school, my mom kept Bill while I worked. Actually, she raised him for a lot longer than that. One day I came home from work to find my mother sitting on her front porch. There she sat, hands covering her face, my son sitting next to her staring off into space. I thought to myself, "This isn't good … this really isn't good!"

I pulled into the driveway, walked up and said, "What's going on, Mom?"

She said, "I just don't know if I can explain it."

I said, "Explain what?"

She said, "Well … Bill was a pistol."

Now, I knew what that meant, but not to what extreme. I sat down with her on the porch and said, "How about you tell me all about it?"

She said, "I was doing the laundry and Bill was playing quietly in the family room. Well, at least that's what I thought he was doing. I came into the kitchen to find all of my canned goods and boxed mixes from the bottom shelves of the pantry on the kitchen floor."

I said, "Well, Mom, I'll go pick them up for you and put them back." I had thought it was going to be a real issue, and I chuckled in relief. She, however, did not chuckle.

She said, in a disbelieving voice, "I am not finished with my story." Getting curious, I told her to go on.

She said, "Not only were the canned goods on the floor along with the boxed mixes, but there are no labels on the cans, the mixes are all out of the boxes. I have pudding packets and no idea what kind they are. I have 20 cans with no idea what's in them. What will I do?"

I said, "Well, tell Daddy every night's dinner will be a surprise."

She said, "I'm not finished with my story!"

Hesitantly, I said, "There's more?"

She said, "He has unloaded all of the bookcases in every room! I pick up one mess and he makes three more! He has unloaded every tissue box and wiped his nose with each and every tissue, and his nose is not running!"

I said, "Well you can re-use them …"

"No! He spit on each one since he couldn't get anything out of his nose!"

"It is OK Mom. I can buy you more boxes of Kleenex."

She said, "I am not finished!"

"OK …" I said hesitantly, "What else?"

"He got his head stuck in the banister on the stairway!"

I said, "Huh?"

She said, "Oh yes! I had to get a jar of Vaseline to lube up his ears to pull his head back through. I almost called the fire department!"

As I sat there listening to this very bad, awful day that my mom was having, I was looking directly into the most beautiful face God ever created on this earth and thinking to myself, "Nahhhh … she has to be imagining these things, right?" Uh, not so much.

Bill was three and it was the week before Christmas. We lived in a small town close to the Mexican border, and Wal-Mart was the place to shop at Christmas time, so there we were. I had just gotten my Christmas bonus and needed to finish shopping for everyone, except Bill. Bill's Christmas presents were neatly wrapped and under the tree. Mom was with us at the back of the store. She had her cart, and I had mine piled as high as I could get it. I was so tired of fighting the crowd I just wanted to check out and go home.

Bill had found the large toy truck aisle and he was on the floor looking at all the trucks. He had pulled out the largest truck and decided it was going home with us. I explained to him that today wasn't the day for him to get gifts. Santa had already gotten all his gifts and today we were shopping for everybody else. I told him it was time to go. At that point, the boy threw himself down on the floor of Wal-Mart, legs and arms sprawled in all directions. He had a death grip on this large red fire truck with a big ladder and he wasn't going anywhere without it.

I said, "Bill, seriously, we need to go. Put the fire truck away, and let's go."

He then commenced a screaming episode of mind-boggling proportion. There was no room for him in the cart, even if I was strong enough to pick him up. I thought to myself, "I have to get to the checkout stand," so I turned to my mother for help with the situation and, lo and behold, the woman had high-tailed it out of the store. I had never seen my mother's backside move that fast!

I turned back to this three year old and thought, "Oh buddy, it's me or you!" I said in my sternest voice, "Get up! March your little behind out of here right now!"

Well, you and I both know my little angel stood right up, saluted me, and marched out of the store immediately, right? Uh, that would be a negative on so many levels. He began to pick up items from the nearest shelves and pitch them at me, yelling, screaming, and throwing what I call a Royal Hissy Fit. At that moment I had to choose between a full shopping cart that represented three exhausting hours of shopping, or the wildly out-of-control three year old kicking and screaming on the floor. It was a tough decision.

I debated, "I can do this…I can take both of them out of here. Yes I can!"

I grabbed my three year old whose legs immediately went into jelly-mode. He refused to stand up, and when I picked him up, he went straight as a board, throwing himself back away from me. I thought to myself, "Really? REALLY? I prayed for THIS?" And in a crowded store within days of Christmas, I heard God, plain as day, "Yes, my child, you did."

I made it out the door with all the Christmas gifts and a screaming three year old in tow. On the way to the car I told him never, NEVER again would I bring him to Wal-Mart. Those days were over! I added that I would only bring him back when he was 18 years old, and that would be to get a job there.

I buckled him into his car seat, crawled into the driver's side, and took a deep breath. Suddenly, from the back seat, I heard his little voice, "Mommy, was I good? Was I good, Mommy?"

And I replied, "Yes, baby, you are good!"

Bill was four the next time I took him anywhere.

Nah, just kidding! Bill and I had what we called "Mommy-Bill Saturdays." It was the day of the week that the two of us could do anything we wanted. We did almost exactly the same thing every Saturday. We drove to a store to buy him an oversized t-shirt for a dollar, then off to the burrito shop, then to the store to buy a bag of peanut M&M's and a video, then home to snuggle in the recliner, watch a movie, and eat the M&Ms wearing the oversized t-shirt.

But one Saturday our routine changed. It was, of course, around Christmas, and Bill and I had been going through some rough patches. His terrible twos had stretched into his threes and now into his fours. This particular day, Bill decided to tell me he hated me and wanted a new mommy. So, off we drove to a nearby mall that had a visiting Santa Claus. The line was very long to see Santa, but we got in line and waited.

Bill looked up at me very angry and said, "What are we DOING here?"

I said, "Well, you see this long line of kids and their moms? This is the line to trade in your mommy for a new mommy. Do you see any you like?"

His eyes got about the size of silver dollars and he said, "No, no, no, Mommy, I want you!"

I said, "Really? 'Cause you told me you want a new mommy."

He said, "Nooooo! I want you; let's go home."

I never heard my son say he wanted a new mommy ever again. Thanks, Santa!

I remember one Sunday at church, one of my friends had a son a year older than Bill. I went to her with tears in my eyes and asked when would these terrible twos, threes and fours ever be over? I went on to explain that one of us went to bed crying every night.

She smiled sweetly and said there would come a time when neither of us would cry. It may only be one day, but soon there would be a day every couple of weeks, and then more and more days would follow. She said to take a picture on that special day when there are no tears, because it would give me hope that better times were ahead. (See the picture at the beginning of this story. Yep, that was us!)

I did take that picture and have it framed in my house. I look at it often because Bill is now a young adult and there have been so many good days. We still eat peanut M&Ms, burritos, and watch movies on Saturday afternoons. God answered my prayer in His own perfect time.

When I remember some of my son's antics in those early days, a smile crosses my face; but these days I look at them through completely different eyes. I have always loved him with an unfailing, tenacious love and have come to see him as the outstanding man I prayed he would become.

Remember the huge temper tantrum in Wal-Mart with the fire truck and ladder? Well, guess what Bill now does for a living? You guessed it! He still loves those big red trucks and ladders reaching to the sky; oh, and his central fire station is right next to - you know it - Wal-Mart! I, for one, truly believe God has a sense of humor!

fireman Bill

Just Debbie ...

When God sits on His porch with His children, I wonder what He sees in us. Does He use the word "pistol" to describe you? Does He say, "I'm not finished with my story yet; there's more ..." Does he go on to tell of strewn boxes and messes that have accumulated from our rebellious actions and attitudes? This, I have to ponder.

Have you ever wondered how God feels about you when you have a really bad, horrible, no good, temper tantrum kind of day?

When I heard Denise tell her story and say the words, "Yes, baby, you are good," I thought, "You're kidding me, right? This kid destroyed Wal-Mart, threw a huge, embarrassing temper tantrum, and went limp as an over-cooked noodle, and you told him he was good? Were you nuts? Obviously this one has never read the book on consistent discipline."

But another part of me was intrigued. What kind of love sees their child's actions through grace versus administering the law? How secure can we feel knowing that we are loved in spite of our most visible failings?

There is a story hidden away in the Old Testament about a woman who throws an adult sized temper tantrum. She ends up trading away everything she knows is right and walking away from her husband to live a very immoral life. This woman's name is Gomer. We could call her "Gomer the Roamer." Not only did her eyes wander, but it appears the rest of her roamed, as well.

Hosea 1:1-11; 3:1-5 tells us how God instructs Hosea to marry Gomer, a prostitute. Even though they had children together, Gomer never chose to remain faithful to Hosea. When God told Hosea to take Gomer as his wife, He also asked him to take the "children of harlotry" as his own. This means the children he raised and loved were probably not even his own.

Perhaps you are wondering why in the world a God who is completely against sin, unfaithfulness, and immorality would ask Hosea to do something that crazy.

Good question. First of all, we never see God asking us to sin or tempting us with evil. That is not who God is. But this was a unique situation and God was sending a very specific message to His people. This is an Abraham and Isaac kind of moment. It is specific, and it is powerful.

Hosea was the prophet God sent to speak to idolatrous, unfaithful Israel. Through His prophet, God was sending a very strong word picture specifically to Israel. He asked His own prophet to model before the people how it would feel to love your wife and repeatedly have to search for her and bring her back while she was still cheating on the husband who loved her.

God, himself, commands Hosea to marry a woman named Gomer. He is told to take for himself an adulterous wife and to conceive children of unfaithfulness, because the land is guilty of the vilest adultery in departing from the Lord." (You can read about this in Hosea 1.) Gomer is described as a prostitute, whore, and a wife of harlotry. In fact, it was difficult to find any translation that had a flattering reference to her. So, you can see why we will simply refer to her as "Gomer the Roamer". (We all get the picture, right? It's much worse than any soap opera.)

God also tells Hosea that Gomer will continue to be unfaithful even after their marriage. God is using Gomer's continual infidelity as a way of demonstrating the continual unfaithfulness of the people of Israel. Hosea is the symbol of God's undying, unending love. God is faithful to us even when we are rebellious, idolatrous, and unfaithful to Him.

So "No Way Hosea" married "Gomer the Roamer". I call him "No Way Hosea" because there was simply no way this man's love was giving up on this woman who so desperately needed redemption.

In Biblical times there were two kinds of prostitutes. There was the kind that made a living by selling themselves just to feed their flesh and their pocket books. But there was an even greater depravity found in the prostitutes who were the harlots found in the pagan temples. Their sexual acts were considered acts of worship to false idols. This was not only immorality but it was also idolatry and blasphemy to God their creator. In all probability, Gomer was both. She represented all of Israel's infidelities and this was utterly detestable to God. We find the culmination of the story in Hosea 3:2 when Hosea pays the slave's price to buy Gomer back. Hosea's name is a variant of the name Joshua, meaning "The Lord Saves." Hosea - Gomer's savior - brings God's stirring message of betrayal and reconciliation to light for the Israelites. God wanted them to know that, even when they were unfaithful, He was faithful. He is a covenant-keeping God.

I don't know about you, but I am glad God saw fit to send us this visual picture. Isn't it comforting to know that our God's love is unconditional? It is not easily angered. He does not give up on us after we repeatedly sin against Him. This woman was as lost as lost could be. She was as ungrateful as she could be. She was a lot like a certain two year old who threatened to trade in his mommy for a new one just because he was having a temper tantrum, but hers was a big one and it lasted for a very long time.

Do you see the connection? I wonder if this is how God feels about me? When I have a really bad, horrible, no good, adult temper tantrum day, does God still look at me with love?

God sees the authentic me - the real me - the one with no make-up, hair that is everywhere, no filters to hide my innermost thoughts. He knows my greatest temptations, my pride, and my hurts. He sees me, too, when I am running away from His love. He knows that, like Gomer, I desperately need His perfect, unconditional, never-ending love, but He also knows I don't even know what that is.

In spite of Gomer and Israel's unfaithfulness, the book of Hosea is filled with hope. There is a tone of God's amazing grace that runs all the way through the entire story. The song lofts throughout the book of Hosea like a Broadway musical with a theme song connecting each and every scene. "Amazing grace, how sweet the sound, that saved a [self-centered, unfaithful, rebellious] wretch like me. I once was lost, but now am found, was blind but now I see."

The truly amazing thing the Bible tells us is that, like Hosea, God truly did buy us back. While we were still in our sins, Christ died for us. We have been redeemed, made right, and considered of great worth, even when we were in the midst of our sins. He did not wait until we were all cleaned up; He tracked us down, picked us up, and carried us right on out of our sinful circumstance.

Like "No Way Hosea", there is absolutely no way God is giving up on you or me; not yesterday, not today, and certainly not tomorrow, no way, Hosea! When He hears me ask, "God was I good today? How can you possibly see anything good in me?"

I hear Him say, "Yes, my child. Through Jesus, you are made perfect."

Now that's very good news for anyone who has recently revisited their terrible twos, twenty-twos, fifty-twos and beyond.

The Gift

"God decided in advance to adopt us into his own family by bringing us to himself through Jesus Christ. This is what he wanted to do, and it gave him great pleasure. So we praise God for the glorious grace he has poured out on us who belong to his dear son."
—*Ephesians 1:5-6 (NLT)*

Christmas family pic

Who is this child? Where did he come from? He is the gift of God, chosen to glorify His Father. Although I could not understand it at the time, God's timing was perfect. God's choice was perfect. Everything God does is always perfect.
--Debbie Sempsrott

You were not just adopted. You were chosen!

Just Debbie …

It was a cold, snowy, Midwest night in the dead of winter. All was perfectly still and the world was blanketed with white. Beautiful snow glistened as far as the eye could see. I lived in the downtown area on an old brick street just a few blocks from Abraham Lincoln's historic home. I was just a high school student at the time and I was enjoying driving myself home in this winter wonderland.

"When all of a sudden I heard such a clatter I sprang to my feet to see what was the matter. And what to my wandering eyes should appear?" (Debbie's version) Nope, I didn't see reindeer, but in front of my car I saw a little white creature covered with glistening snow and two little eyes peering at me.

I jumped out of my car, scooped up this frightened little grey and white dog, and took her home with me. My folks weren't awake so the coast was clear. I decided I needed to warm up this little pup and we had no dog food. "So," I thought, "What would I like if I were a dog? Never mind that, what would I like?"

I love honey buns warm from the oven, so I baked one for me and one for my new friend. I also gave her some warm milk.

The next day my brother asked me what I was going to name her and I said, "Hmm ... how about Honey Bun?"

He said, "There is no way on God's green earth that I am going outside and yelling "Honey Bun!" So I named her Gretchen.

We tried to find her original family but could not. We wondered why anyone would not want this darling little dog. Then, for Mother's Day, my mother found her present waiting for her down in our finished basement. On her couch were five little puppies who were birthed right there. Surprise! Happy Mother's Day, indeed! She got a new couch and we got puppies.

My parents will tell you that cute little puppies were not all I brought home. I also brought people home with me, lots of people. I had a best friend in elementary school and her parents were going through a divorce which was hard on her, so I brought her home with me every day after school.

My nickname has always been "Julie" after the cruise director from the "Love Boat" so I have always planned the fun, the cruise, the tour, the parties, and the mischief!

My father was a pastor. If that wasn't enough, both of my grandpas were ministers. My grandma had to wear a dress everywhere she went and there was "no dancin', drinkin', or card playin'." Life was serious and pastors' kids were supposed to behave. "Supposed to" is the key thought here. The only problem was, I preferred to play. I was supposed to do chores and set a good example. I tried hard to be good, but I was so gifted in the play department!

I hung out with the other pastors' and elders' kids, which is where I am sure I got many of my best ideas for mischief. At least, that is the story I stuck to. One of those elder's kids came up with the idea of putting tacks in the baptistery. I have never seen anyone in all my life get so excited, jumping up and down, about their decision. That was when I learned the waders the pastors wear can get holes in them. Oops!

Not only was I comfortable at my church, but church camp was my second home. I grew up as a church camper and was the camp lifeguard in high school. My Dad was the dean for a week of camp every summer.

One week at camp it had rained all week long and things were pretty boring, so I thought I would spice things up a bit. The pool was closed, and due to the heavy rains, there were no sports. I decided a good mud slide would be just the thing to pick up everyone's spirits, especially mine. So, I started at the top of the hill and slid all the way down to the bottom, and into the lake I went. This was so much fun, I did it again and again, and soon I had a large group of followers. They don't call me "Julie" for nothing. Before you knew it, there was a whole group of us that looked like the "Blue Man Group" only it was more like the "brown camper group." It was then I heard a voice booming from the heavens, but it was not my Heavenly Father calling. Guess who the camp dean was that week?

Not only did I love a good party as a kid, I decided to become a teacher. That is a built-in party every day, right? My very first year of teaching was at the Christian school where I had graduated. Can you believe they would hire me to come back there?

Obviously they were not privy to the tacks in the baptistery fiasco!

My first year of teaching was like Heaven on earth to me. I taught kindergarten in the morning and PE for all grades in the afternoon. I also worked with their music ensembles and extra-curricular sports. Boy, was this the job for me! I got paid to teach kids music, play tennis, golfing, swimming, bowling and cheerleading. It was a match made in Heaven!

The truth is, I have always been a kid at heart, and I love to hang out with kids. I took care of campers and students, and love my niece and nephew. I have been asked many times to be a godparent, but what about having someone to take home that was my very own?

After 14 years of marriage there was no party to plan and no more mischief to make. How could I be the one with no child of my own while people much younger had a whole team? Perhaps someone reading this knows what I am talking about? We went through tests and procedures, and even a few losses. I finally agreed to a surgery, and we prayed

Maybe you can understand why I love the story of Hannah so much. The Bible tells us she prayed that God would give her a son someday. She told the Lord that if He did, she would give that boy back to Him. Can you imagine agreeing to that?

I can, because I did!

God set us on the path toward adoption. We were selected to be the parents of a little baby boy. The nursery was finished and his name was hanging on the wall. All was ready for his arrival. He was to fly in soon and we were so anxious to receive our baby. The party was just about to begin when we received the call. The grandparents had decided to keep him. That baby was not the one for us.

I went back to the Christian school where I was teaching and everyone knew about our disappointment. The one thing that may be even more difficult to deal with than heartache is the well-meaning sympathy of friends; the sad looks of pity and uncomfortably awkward condolences. There was nowhere to hide and no place to run.

That year my principal and his wife, who were wonderful friends, prayed that God would, indeed, give us the gift of a family. A short time later one of the families from the school approached us. They had heard about our loss. God's timing is always perfect!

As a result of that meeting, we met our birthmother. She told me she felt the baby she was carrying would be a "David" filled with song, like in the Bible. She wanted him to be raised around music and sports. Boy, did she call that one right! That still amazes me today.

This young lady selected us. We were chosen. God picked a baby for us who looked so much like his cousins that people cannot believe he is adopted. He is musical beyond belief and athletic to the max. Perhaps he will even beat his father in golf one day.

How does God do these things? That baby is now a wonderful young man who leads worship like King David. He is passionate for God. I have always known that he was on loan to us and really belongs to God, his Heavenly Father. This boy has been able to sing solos like an angel since he was three years old; he learned to play guitars and drums without a lesson.

Who is this child? Where did he come from? He is the gift of God, chosen to glorify His Father. God's timing was perfect. God's choice was perfect. Everything God does is always perfect.

Let me share with you what I mean. On July 30th I went to dinner with my entire family to celebrate my birthday. I received a call at dinner from our birth mother. She said, "Happy Birthday! I am in labor. Now don't hurry. There is no rush. Eat your dinner.

Open your presents. Enjoy your cake. We will call back when it is time."

There is a picture of me blowing out the candles when the phone rings again. She said, "Happy Birthday, I will have a special delivery for you soon." So my husband and I took off for the hospital. We were there for our son's birth and I was the very first person to hold him. What an amazing birthday gift! There will never be another gift that will ever come close to that sacrificial gift of love. I can only imagine how Mary and Joseph felt.

Each year at Christmas as I see the little baby and all the gifts, I am reminded that God gave his son so that we could be adopted. We were chosen! We are wanted! Our gifts, our soul, and the timing of our lives are ordained by God. There is no chance; there is only choice.

"For God so loved the world that He gave His one and only son." (John 3:16a NIV)

Every year on my birthday and on Mother's Day I give thanks for Susan, a very special birth mom. She not only gave my son life, she gave a life to my son. Adoption can be challenging for a child to understand. My son has had the privilege of meeting his birth mom and half-sisters. It was a blessed day, and an emotionally difficult one for all of us.

Last year I made a tough decision for me, personally. I invited his birth mom and half-sisters to come meet him on his turf. I wanted them to actually get to see him lead worship for our church as his birth mom had a dream of music for his life before he was ever born. I must admit that this day was a little awkward at first, but it was a turning point.

I say it was a tough day for one reason, and one reason alone. You see, this boy is wanted and loved. He has felt like mine, alone, all of his life. There has never been a birth father in the scene so there are no comparisons for my husband to deal with. But there have always been two moms – sharing, loving, and praying. One gave life to him, and one has shared his life, but we have always shared him in our hearts.

I know his birth mom has loved him, grieved over the loss of him, and kept track of him. She has always longed for the day she could finally meet him again. I must be honest and tell you that, as much as I planned this day – bought her a special portrait of him, and wanted my son to feel complete – it was the hardest day of my life.

Eighteen years ago she gave me the best present imaginable, but on this day I opened my heart to say to her, "Here's our boy. You can get to know him."

It was scary, risky, and heart wrenching. I knew how much she loved him; yet she couldn't raise him. What if he chose to love her more than me? (I'm just being painfully honest here.) I had to take that risk, in faith, because I needed this special young man to know how much he is loved, not by just one mom, but by two.

This young woman made mistakes, but in spite of all she went through she had chosen life for this baby. She had prayed for this baby and loved him, although she was unable to keep him. This incredibly special young woman had spent her life working to get healthy, and had gone to school to help others who had faced what she had been through. I wanted our son to know about her love, her courage, and her healing because of God's great mercy. I knew they must meet again, and yet I knew of his struggles because he was adopted.

I would like for you to hear what my son, Chad, has to say about adoption.

Theme for English 12, as written by Chad

The instructor said,
Go home and write a page tonight.
And let that page come out of you,
Then it will be true—I wonder if it's that simple.

I am eighteen, white, and was born in Santa Ana, California.
I've been to many schools but now I ended up at
Southwest High School.
I see myself as a human, not a majority or minority.
I love to smile, laugh, play music, and play sports.
I like to spend time with those who enjoy my presence,
Those people make me feel special, like I matter.
Does everyone matter?
Matter to someone?
I don't know . . . I would like to think so.
It hurts me to think that people feel they don't matter.

I was hurt when I found out I was adopted.
Why was I given up?
What was wrong with me?
What did I do wrong?
I continued to ask these questions,
But were these the right questions?
Why wasn't I asking … Why did they choose me?
Did they know me?
Did they have my life mapped out?
But eventually, most importantly, I would ask,
How did I end up being so lucky with these amazing parents?

I have one sister, and I love her more than any other
Teenager would love a sister.
My sister is special to a lot of people.
To me, she's Chelsea.
She loves life, laughing, and being happy.

My life is not ordinary, but then again whose life is?
Life is learning from mistakes.
I have lived a lot of "life" and will continue to make mistakes.
So I will continue to live life as I have been
With a smile on my face and nothing holding me back.

Those words are from my son, Chad. I love his writing, his singing, his sense of humor, his smile, and his hugs. In fact, I love everything about him - except the way he cleans his room (or doesn't). Actually, he is a born leader; he gets his sister to clean for him. This young man is a true blessing to us, always!

I truly believe it is important that I share with you the rest of this story. My son has just married, and he will in the near future be a father himself. This is an unending story of grace learned, received, and given. I need to tell you that on his wedding day he danced with both of his mothers. First he danced with the one who gave him life and then he danced with the one who shared his life with him. It was unpretentious, perfect, and it was just as God had always intended. Chad's two half-sisters were also there; one of them, along with her husband and newborn baby, drove fourteen hours to come and share in his wedding day. It was unbelievably special to have all of them sitting there with us. We talked, laughed, and were all proud of this young man. I do believe Chad has come a long way from the day he wrote his poem. He not only knows he was adopted; he now knows that he was always loved, chosen, and is special to his entire family, friends, and church. Only God can pull off something as amazing, healing, and joyful as that!

This year I am, once again, reminded of the story of Hannah. The special gift God gave us is now a man. He is heading out to begin his life as a husband and father, and he wants to be a worship leader. (I have known that was his calling from the first night I heard his little lungs.) Like Hannah, I am trying to hand him back to God so he can be used as God intended. Now I read Hannah's story with new understanding. (I bet she wanted to live right there in the temple. Hmm…not a bad idea!) Once again, like Hannah, I am reminded that this child is a gift from God that is just on loan to us. He truly belongs to His Heavenly Father, and was placed here on earth to serve Him. I want to give him my love and blessing, and give him wings to fly, and so I write these words to my amazing son:

Dear Chad,

It is God who gave life to you, and your birthmother gave you to your father and me. Most importantly, she gave you back to God for His use from the moment of your birth. She knew before you were even born that God would use you. There has never been a day that you have been unwanted. You have always been a gift from God. There has never been a moment that we did not know this truth. Your father and I have been blessed beyond measure.

I love you, my son. I am proud of you beyond words. I want you to know that you are a complete Gift

*from God. You were not just adopted. You were chosen!
You will always be ours and you will always be His. A
part of you belongs to a very special young lady who gave
life to you and prayed for you to be exactly who you are
today. I am so thankful for her courageous gift. You did
not grow in my stomach, you grew in my heart, and that
is where you will always be. I return you to the God
who gave you to me, and I know that you will always
make our God proud.*

*You are adopted by God, chosen for His glory,
equipped for God's good pleasure. I see you leading
worship and using the amazing gifts that God has
given you. I see you as a leader, an amazing husband
and father, and always a beloved son. To me you are*
"The Gift"!

Chad Sempsrott

The Waiting Room

"Whether you turn to the right or to the left, your ears will hear a voice behind you, saying, 'This is the way; walk in it'."—Isaiah 30:21 (NIV)

An elevator stuck between floors, a doctor's office packed with people, a group of people huddled in a corner before a storm, a courtroom jammed with people waiting for a verdict. What do all of these scenarios have in common? The silence is deafening. All are waiting for an outcome for which they are not prepared; stuck in a space somewhere between the pages of their life. The end of the book will not be determined until we see what they do during this life-changing interruption in their otherwise normal lives. Perhaps there has been a point when you have found yourself stuck somewhere in-between.

--Debbie Sempsrott

Funny Denise …

It was February and I had just turned 36 years old. I had scheduled my yearly exam. You see, I was trying to get pregnant again. I had tried for over seven years to get pregnant and finally had my son at the age of 30. I wanted another child and my clock was ticking pretty fast. Every year it was the same story, "Everything looks good, no issues, you're just trying too hard, relax!" Geeze, if I heard that one more time I would scream! And yet, I wished I had heard it this time.

Ahead of schedule, I walked into the doctor's office and sat calmly in the waiting room for over an hour. When my name was called I walked in only to be humiliated by being asked to stand on the scales to weigh myself. Dreading the inevitable, like a prisoner facing a firing squad, I put my purse down, took my shoes off, pulled off my sweater, looked at the nurse and asked politely if I could just strip naked to get better numbers. She always said no! I started to step on the scale and as I placed my big toe on the scale - I always like to sneak up on it - she immediately ran the scale up to the one hundred and fifty pound mark. I backed off and scowled at her. She looked frightened.

"How about you back that scale down to a hundred pounds? What makes you think I weigh a hundred and fifty pounds before I ever get on there?"

She quickly moved the weight marker to a hundred pounds. I stepped up ever so gently so I would not frighten the scale, and she slowly bumped it up…one-ten, one-twenty, one-thirty, one-forty, one-fifty…and the bar never moved! She looked at me disgustedly as I said, "I never said I didn't weigh over a hundred and fifty pounds, I just didn't want you to assume I did before I stepped on the scale!"

She took me to the room, gave me the paper doll clothes and asked me to put them on saying the doctor would be in shortly to examine me. I so wish paper doll clothes had tags. I never know which way to put them on - open in the front or open in the back?

This particular day I decided to open it in the front but I tied the bottom corners together to make a lovely top. I wrapped the bottom half around me like a skirt and then I modeled my outfit in front of the mirror on the back of the door. Woo Hoo! I looked fabulous! I was so proud of myself until the door opened while I was modeling and in walked the doctor. He was speechless.

He asked me to sit down so he could start the examination. I went to sit down on the exam table and apparently the skirt I made was a tad too tight as it ripped from aft to stern!

The doctor began to examine me from the top floor to the bottom floor, as usual. I compare a breast exam to being in an elevator. You aren't looking at him, he's not looking at you, you're staring at the ceiling and he's, well, you get the idea. It is the most awkward feeling. So I figure if it's awkward for me, why shouldn't I share that feeling with the doctor?

"So, Doc, find anything yet?"

He said, "Nope."

I said, "Yep, that's what my husband says, he can't find them either!"

That joke always worked with my other doctors, but this time was different - way different. All of a sudden, he asked me to sit up and he felt my underarm, too. I got concerned and the concern turned to fear as he told me I had a lump. I needed to get it checked out. He was scheduling me for a mammogram and he wanted it done right away.

"Get a mammogram at my age? Are you kidding me? I am 36 years old with a six year old son to raise. I don't have time for lumps!"

The drive home was awful. I was scared. I was angry. I was fearful, to say the least.

A couple of days later, I went in for the first of many mammograms. I want to find the man who came up with that contraption and attach one of his body parts to it. I walked in and the lady doing the mammogram was so sweet. She said, "Take your clothes off, put on the gown opened to the front (guess the doctor called ahead) and come out when you are ready."

I did and found myself standing in front of this harmless looking machine...wrong!

She told me to lift and place my offering on the altar. On a good day I am an "A" cup, but this wasn't one of those days. I smiled at her and said, "Hun, do you want me to lift my stomach, too, so I can get something to offer as a sacrifice?"

She smiled and said, "No, this is just fine. Lean into the plate and it will work."

I leaned in and she grabbed what little loose skin I had and pulled and tugged. I heard the machine hum and down came this other plate. I backed up quickly.

I took a look at her and said, "WHAT are you DOING?"

She said, "Hold still, I am going to take a picture now."

I replied, "Well get the Polaroid out and I will stand still but you are not smashing my parts in that machine!"

"Yes ma'am, I am. Now step back over here and let's try this again."

With trepidation I paused for thought and then walked slowly back over to her. Again she pulled and tugged and finally got enough of me in the machine so she could take a picture.

After taking the right side she moved to the left. She actually was a tad bit happier as that is my bigger side. It's likely to be a "B" cup - oh, who am I kidding? It's a large "A" cup. She told me to lean into the machine, raise my arm up over the machine and place my offering on the altar. I said in my best southern accent, "Honey child, if I raise my arm up over this here machine, these here parts will retreat into my armpits. You can tug and pull all you want but it ain't hap'nin, Cap'n!" She finally shook her head and told me to just lean in as far as I could so she could get a good picture.

Waiting on the results for three days was excruciating. I remember when the doctor called and said they wanted to do a needle biopsy on my lump as soon as possible. I wanted to crawl into a hole and say no more. I wanted to hear them say it's not cancer, but all they would tell me was, "We don't know what it is but this next test will show us."

It didn't. The answer I got after two weeks of worrying was, "We aren't sure what it is. We can't rule out cancer so we are just going to watch it."

Watch it?! Really? You are certified doctors and you can't tell me what it is?

I couldn't believe what I was hearing. And then the lamest comment to ever come out of a doctor's mouth, "Don't worry about anything until we tell you that you need to worry."

So, for two years I got mammograms every six months, and for two years they would send me for more tests because of that lump, and for two years they wouldn't tell me anything except, "Don't worry until we tell you to worry."

After two years, I told the doctor, "Take it out. If it's cancer, take off my breast. Don't wake me up to ask me, just take it off!"

I went home and told my husband what was happening; that the tumor was the size of a ping pong ball and they were going to remove it. I couldn't wait around to see if it was going to turn cancerous; I wanted it out!

He took me in his arms, kissed my cheek and said, "Sweetheart, ya know I love ya right?" He continued, "You know I never married you for your breasts, right? So whatever happens I am good with it."

I fell so in love with him when he said that. Then he looked at me with those big hazel eyes, smiled at me and said, "But darlin' if you get replacements, make them a "D" cup, would ya, please?"

Ya gotta love a redneck. They speak from the heart.

They removed that tumor and my large "A" cup went down to match my almost "A" cup. It wasn't malignant and it would not have turned cancerous. I thank God every day for that blessing. However, in those two long years, I planned my funeral and wrote my will. The fear that came over me would have been what took my life, not the illness.

Just Debbie ...

I don't know about you, but I don't like waiting. Sitting in a doctor's waiting room or in a hospital waiting room is the worst. For me, it's even worse than wearing the cute little paper clothes when you get to the main event.

Did you know there are even waiting rooms on cruise ships? Somehow, I never considered this possibility until I ended up there one time. Up to that point I had filled every day with buffets, pools, shows, shopping, music, and room service. Life was glorious and breathtaking. I never dreamed I would spend the rest of my cruise waiting to get out of quarantine before I could see blue skies again. Life often happens while we are making other plans. I caught a serious virus that was an on-board epidemic. My cruise came with a no refund policy. I was dreaming of shows - not shots; buffets - not buckets; and ocean breezes - not the queasies. Sometimes life is a lot like that. It feels unfair. The waiting feels really long.

If the truth be told, none of us likes waiting. We get impatient waiting too long for our favorite fast food; we get anxious waiting for answers when life seems uncertain and we crave answers and reassurance. But there are lessons to be learned in God's waiting room.

As a matter of fact, I find myself sitting in God's big waiting room right now. I am sitting on my couch working on this story and thinking of even more questions that remain unanswered at this time. When we started writing this book, all was well with me, but as timing would have it, I am presently the one sitting in the waiting room. It's not nearly as funny as the beginning of this story. With time and perspective, stories often become humorous. I presently lack both. When we are in the midst of something, our perspective is usually, "Just get me out of here, now!"

I recently went back to the doctor to get the stitches removed from a chunk they took out of my arm. They said if there was an issue I would hear back in just a few days. The pathology reports could take ten days to two weeks. Two weeks later I still had no results. At dinner time I got a call from the doctor's receptionist. I thought she was reminding me about my stitches. Instead, she said, "The doctor would like you to come in tomorrow morning to meet with you about your pathology report."

"Oh shoot … that didn't sound good." She wouldn't tell me anything more.

My friends reminded me that the longer the wait, the better the news. I walked into the room and was working at feeling confident when the doctor said, "I have good news and bad news. The good news is that I am really glad we took it out the day I saw it. The bad news is, it is cancer and I want you to see a surgical dermatologist as soon as possible. They will need to get clear margins and it will probably need to be bigger."

As he drew a circle on my arm, I drew a blank.

The word "cancer" and your name should never be used in the same sentence. Never! No matter which part of your body it has invaded, it is an unwelcome guest. I was thinking, "Which kind of cancer is this? Does it grow and spread?"

I guess I think of it like this: You live in your home filled with your furniture and decorations. It feels safe and homey. Then one day someone breaks into your house. It doesn't matter what they steal from you. The fact that a stranger has been in your home invaded your life and violated your safe place, takes away your peace. You have a new realization for the first time in that moment, your life and safety can be taken away from you. The truth is that we all need reminders of God's faithful mercy toward us from time to time.

Many of the great Old Testament characters of faith were remembered for building stone monuments to God and naming them. God knew they would need tangible signs to remind them of his faithfulness to them as it is easy for us to forget. Every time they would pass by a certain town, such as Bethel, they would be reminded by seeing the stone altar they left there after an encounter with the living God.

In Genesis 22:14 Abraham built an altar as he was about to offer his son as a sacrifice in obedience to the Lord's request. Abraham named the altar "Jehovah Jirah" which means "God will provide." In Abraham's most difficult hour, when he faced losing what he loved the most in this life - his son - Abraham chose to stop and build an altar to God.

In Genesis 33:20 we see Jacob building an altar at Bethel. The altar he built is called "El Bethel" meaning "God appeared" to him there. Moses' altar to God in Exodus 17:15 is named "The Lord is my Banner." A banner is a symbol of victory over the enemy. Gideon's altar is referred to as "The Lord is Peace." In I Samuel 7:12 we see that Samuel took a stone and set it up as an altar that he called "Ebenezer" which means "Stone of Help."

Why did these great servants of God build altars? An altar is a place where one *lays it all down* before God. These people of God were considered great simply because of their faith.

One of the most spectacular Bible stories involves an altar, a prophet, and a large group of false prophets of Baal. The story of the prophet, Elijah, is recorded for us in I Kings 18:36-39. This was definitely a show down at the "Not OK Corral". I say this because the Israelites were definitely not OK. They were wavering big time.

To give us a little background on this we see Elijah talking to the people in I Kings 18:21 (NKJV). "And Elijah came to all the people, and said, 'How long will you falter between two opinions? If the Lord is God, follow Him; but if Baal, follow him.' But the people answered him not a word." Elijah goes on in verse 22 to say, "I alone am left a prophet of the Lord."

The sides are drawn. Baal's prophets were four hundred and fifty men strong against one man, plus a mighty God! So Elijah takes twelve stones to build his altar to God. There is one stone for each of the tribes of Israel. So far, so good, but now comes the shocking part. God is being asked to send down fire from above. Elijah begins dumping pots of water all over the sacrificial wood which would make it impossible to catch on fire. He doesn't just do this one time, he does it three times. The wood is drenched, soaking wet. He is not only standing all alone, he is completely outnumbered by the enemy, and now everything is wet.

Elijah begins to pray, "Lord God of Abraham, Isaac, and Israel, let it be known this day that You are God in Israel and I am Your servant, and that I have done all these things at Your word. Hear me, O Lord, hear me, that this people may know that You are the Lord God, and that You have turned their hearts back to You again." (1 Kings18:36 NKJV) This was some gutsy praying and it preceded one of the most exciting encounters in the entire Bible.

I Kings 18:38 goes on to tell us that the fire of the Lord did fall. It consumed the sacrifice, the wood, the stones, the dust, and licked up all the water that was in the trench. When the people saw this they fell on their faces saying, "The Lord, He is God!" (vs. 39)

I guess you could say Elijah got to kick some Baal Booty that day. He only had a team of two against a big old ugly team of four hundred and fifty. However, Elijah played for the original Angel's team that day, and when God gets up to bat, the game always gets exciting.

The story is simply unforgettable, but it is also remarkable because of what happens after this amazing sweeping victory. When the prophets of Baal threaten to take the Prophet Elijah's life, he runs, panics, and whines like a baby. This very same man just whooped four hundred and fifty big bad prophets, but he is afraid of one really bad woman who has it out for him. I don't know how you feel about this little twist of events, but I am personally thankful because it gives me hope. We aren't the only ones who can be on the mountain top one day and in the ditch the next.

Although Elijah saw that God was faithful, powerful, and overwhelmingly sovereign, he found himself forgetting the victory and focusing on the fear. We tend to focus on the tree versus seeing the entire forest. When we are sick, it seems bigger, longer, and more overwhelming than anything else at that time. When we feel lonely, we tend to forget all of the times we have been blessed with love and fellowship. When the obstacles are great, our faith needs tangible reminders.

Right now, I am sitting in the doctor's waiting room, and I have a few things hanging over my head. I am reminded that we never know our future, but we know who holds our future. Today, I am remembering all the ways God has been faithful to me in the past.

Like Elijah, I recently had my own little experience with water. This past week my mind was elsewhere. My heart was really asking God, "Are you here right now with me? Do you care about my little world and struggles?" As I was in the process of writing this story I had a most unusual thing happen. I went to Target shopping. Now, on a good day I have trouble remembering where I parked. On a good day, I can walk outside and have a feeling that tells me to turn left or right and start looking. Obviously, this was not one of my better days as I walked outside and had ... well, nothing! It was over a hundred degrees outside; I had a cart full of stuff and absolutely no idea where my car was parked. I did remember which car I had brought, that was a plus. By the time I finally found my car I was hot, and my bandaged arm was itching. My mind was elsewhere - certainly not there - and I went off and left my case of bottled water under my shopping cart.

That evening, I began telling my story to a group of ladies who were all sitting around my table. I told them about how I had left their water under my cart. One of the ladies sitting there stood up waving her arms. She was very excited about something, I just wasn't sure what. She began telling us how she had pulled into a parking spot at Target and noticed that some crazy lady had left an entire case of water under it - yep, that crazy woman would be me. She had taken the water, put it in her car, and told her husband about her little find. She had also brought this case of water to my house that night, and promptly went outside and carried it in. I decided to build my own little altar that day and call it "The Target of living water."

When life gets tough, our perspective gets foggy - kind of like my parking lot search-a-thons - and we need to remember to lay it all down. Even in those times, God surrounds us with fellow journeyers to help pick up our pieces (and water).

Although we would all agree that no one enjoys sitting in a waiting room, God can accomplish mighty things with just a few stones, lots of water, and one faithful person who is willing to just be still and wait on Him.

It is in the waiting room of life that we find something we may not have realized before ... our God is there waiting for us. Denise jokingly asked the nurse about "laying her offering on the altar." But she really was on the right track. No matter how private the struggle, how embarrassing your situation, or how long your wait, God is there with you. If He could defeat four hundred and fifty evil warriors with one man's prayer and a little water, just think what He can do for you. Even Elijah was scared of one strong, bold, evil woman. He ran like the wind from her. What amazing strength we women possess, for good or evil!

When we give our weakness, worry, and waiting to God, and are willing to lay it all down on the altar, we will see a glimpse of God's glory shining through the dark clouds that surround us. Our waiting room is merely God's preview of a fine Broadway Play. Our waiting often attracts the attention of those around.

They are merely onlookers, waiting, watching, and observing how we will handle what has come our way. After all of the acts are over and we reach the final scene, the music begins to climax and it is time for the great reveal. Will this all make sense? Who will receive the glory, adoration, and applause?

It is at precisely this moment we are called to bend our knee, bow our head, and believe in a God that is bigger, wiser, and beyond our understanding. He reaches down and takes our hand. The waiting is over. The God of the universe takes our pain upon Himself; He takes our mess and reveals His message!

Perhaps, it seems to you that your wait has been way too long. I understand exactly how you feel. We all know the feeling, the aching and the longing that we experience in God's waiting room. It can shake us to the core, and break us down.

"An elevator stuck between floors, a doctor's office packed with people, a group of people huddled in a corner before a storm, a courtroom jammed with people waiting for a verdict; what do all of these scenarios have in common? The silence is deafening, all are waiting for an outcome for which they are not prepared; stuck in a space somewhere between the pages of their lives.

The rest of the story will be determined by the choices we make in response to the life-changing interruptions that come our way. Only faith can transform a waiting room into an altar of praise.

Her Father's Eyes

"But God chose the foolish things of
the world to shame the wise;
God chose the weak things of the world to shame the strong."
--I Corinthians 1:27 (NIV)

One time my daughter was telling me something
very insightful and I was trying to figure out how
she would know this and why she was telling me.
She merely said, "I have my Father's eyes."
Astonishing! She has said this to me on more than one
occasion and I have listened, marveled, believed and
obeyed. This sweet girl truly has her Father's Eyes!
--Debbie Sempsrott

The Weak made Strong

Funny Denise . . .

I met her at church. She was standing in the front row; arms raised high to God, eyes toward heaven, singing her heart out. She was praising God in a way that I only dreamed of praising my Father. She was in His presence and she wasn't at all concerned with who was standing around her, if they were staring at her, or what they were thinking about her. She was having a conversation with her Father. It was hard not to witness the beauty of her love for her Father without a huge smile on your face or tears in your eyes.

Chelsea is Debbie's daughter and she has Down syndrome. I have seen people with Down syndrome but never had any kind of relationship with them. It's a shame to only find out later in my life that, until now, I had missed out on the purest form of love there will ever be, next to God Himself. I have always thought of Chelsea as having the love of God, and perhaps being the truest form of an angel that exists here on earth. I have never seen Chelsea angry in all the years I have known her. However, I have seen Chelsea sad.

Chelsea and I have a lot in common. We both have tummy issues. We both must watch what we eat as we get sick pretty easily. So Chelsea and I have had a lot of quality bathroom time together. Most of the time it's Chelsea who has the issues, so

Debbie and I make sure at least one of us is in the restroom with her at all times to ensure all is well. If I am in there with her, I usually try to help her by softly asking how she is doing, and if not well, telling her to breathe in through her nose and out through her mouth to relax her muscles and help her get through it. Sometimes we have little chats while waiting and it keeps her mind busy so she doesn't begin to cry.

One particular Saturday, Debbie, Chelsea and I had gone to Yuma for lunch and a little bit of shopping. My stomach was causing me problems most of the day, and during lunch the time finally came for a bathroom break. I excused myself from the table and started down the aisle to the restroom when I felt this little hand grab mine and heard the voice of an angel saying, "It's OK. I will go with you and it'll be OK."

We got to the bathroom and there was a long line. I finally made it into a stall and told Chelsea to keep her hand on the top of the door so I would know where she was at all times. As I started focusing on the job at hand, I noticed Chelsea's fingers on the top of the stall door. She was waving and pointing at me, and then I heard a giggle that could only be Chelsea's. It's so contagious that no matter what you are doing at the time, you can't help but chuckle, yourself. I glanced at the space between the door and the hinge and there she was, one eye peeping in at me with this enormous grin on her face. I smiled back and said, "It will be a few more minutes Chelsea, I just don't feel so good right now." Looking back, I should have remained quiet because it started a conversation that will, I hope, forever remain unmatched.

With a bathroom full of women - every stall filled - I began to hear these precious words from Chelsea, "It's going to be alright! Just breeeeeathe in through your nose and out your mouth and pushhhhh! Push really, really hard! Gruntttt like this … Erggggggg! Is it coming? Do you feel it? You will be able to feel it, I promise! Is it out yet? Does your tummy hurt? Rub your tummy with your hands, it will help. Keep pushing … keep grunting … Erggggg!!"

The bathroom was quiet - deathly quiet; no flushing, no water running, no conversation except the one-way conversation from Miss Chelsea trying to help me. All I wanted to do was get out of there. As I walked sheepishly out of my little cubicle, Chelsea let out a big "Woo-Hoo you did it! I am so proud of you!"

I got a standing ovation from every woman in that bathroom, so I did what any other woman in that position would do. I took a bow, and so did Chelsea. Chelsea and I truly have our own language of love.

Just Debbie …

Denise's story just about covers it. That's my special girl and I'm proud of her!

Right after her birth, I had a good friend named Linda who came to visit. She said, "Debbie, you may not understand what I am going to say right now, but Chelsea is going to be the greatest blessing in your life."

I said, "You are right, I don't understand." I didn't understand anything right then.

I met Linda about a year before Chelsea was born. She was the foster parent of five special needs girls and she had adopted two girls. She had lost a daughter with Down syndrome at the age of twelve. This loss broke her heart, but opened her life to walk through this new door to care for other special needs kids that other people could not care for. I have been in Linda's home many times and it is like sitting on a set from *Country Living* magazine. It is so peaceful and often comes with some yummy baked treat that you would see in a magazine.

God allowed me to observe Linda with her pew full of special needs girls at church every Sunday for about a year. They were a hoot! Linda's smile warms up everything around her. I thought it was all pretty amazing. She had modeled something special for me that I would soon need to know; but I had no idea my day was coming.

The truly remarkable thing is that Linda was actually invited to our church by my prayer partner, Shelly. My prayer partner and I met every week to walk around a lake and pray. She knew we were praying to have children and she was praying for me. In the midst of this, she invited Linda to church.

Can you fathom how the God of the universe is so sovereign that one year before I would personally encounter the world of special needs, He would send me my very own lifeline? When God gets ready to work in a person's life, He uses ordinary people. This time God used my prayer partner; she was not only praying for me, she was used by God to intervene for me without even knowing how her obedience would change my life. This intervention is beyond comprehension to me.

Our long-awaited baby boy was born on Sunday, July 31st at about 2:00 a.m. We took him home from the hospital that Sunday evening. The interesting thing is, I had a doctor's appointment the very next morning. So, off to the doctor I went with my brand new baby who had only been with me for about twelve hours. My prayer partner, Shelly, accompanied me to this infamous doctor's appointment.

The doctor had on plaid pants, a striped shirt, and a very busy tie. I realized I was sleep-deprived and began to wonder if my eyes were playing tricks on me, as this man looked like a character from Dr. Seuss's "Green Eggs and Ham". I was scared ... very scared!

I had not slept for two nights. Just twenty-four hours prior to this appointment, we were at the hospital for the birth of our son. In the delivery room with our birthmother who was in labor, I was eating Wheat Thins, trying not to be sick, and now here I was with the doctor of the Seussical plaid pants. My brand new baby boy began to cry and my friend, Shelly, asked where she could find his bottle.

I had a bad case of brain freeze. "*Hmmmm*, do we really need one of those?" The thought had not crossed my mind to pack a bottle. Shelly hustled out to find some formula. That was just the warm-up act. The next part is where it gets really exciting.

The doctor calls me in and as I am holding my one-day-old baby boy in my arms, what he says seems to come out in slow motion.

"Congratulations! You're p-r-e-g-n-a-n-t! Who's this cute little boy?"

"Ummm, this is my brand new baby, and it sounds like he is getting a little sis." Now, this doctor was not telling me something I did not know - hence the Wheat Thins in the delivery room; however, that day it became oh, so real!

That night was meet-the-new-baby night at our house. I invited my entire family over for dinner and a meet-and-greet. Before we blessed the food, I said, "I am so glad that you could all come, but before we eat I just need to share one little thing with you. (Wait for it. It's the slow motion thing again!) This is our baby boy and he is going to be a big brother soon because I'm P-r-e-g-n-a-n-t!"

My entire family laughed loud and hard. No, they howled! It would be double the blessing, double the joy. The funny and awkward part was when I was pregnant and carrying a newborn. People would look at me, then him, and then my stomach, and then back at him. They really were not sure what to ask. It was great fun. We all knew what they were thinking, "Isn't it time for this girl to be over the pickles and ice cream thing?" They were sorely mistaken!

Chelsea made her entry into this world six weeks early and was a little preemie, weighing only four and half pounds at birth. I went in to see my doctor because I had not been feeling well. My vision kept breaking up and I was seeing "gold." Unfortunately, it was not from 'them thar' California gold mines. It was from Toxemia, or Preeclampsia, caused by pregnancy-induced high blood pressure believed to be related to a calcium deficiency. They began checking the baby's vital signs, but couldn't get any readings. They rushed me across the street to the hospital where they were able to get things stabilized for a while. The next morning, the same thing happened again. My levels went sky high and they lost the baby's levels altogether.

I had an emergency C-section before the epidural could even kick-in. That is the main reason I decided that any future additions would need to be through adoption or delivery by stork. The doctor would later tell me that Chelsea and I had both been saved by miraculous intervention. I knew God had rescued us and that she was His little blessing to me.

The Toxemia continued to raise my blood pressure for a couple of weeks. The first few days after her birth, I was still pretty unaware of anything going on around me. My baby was in ICU and I was not able to have visitors. After a few days I remember looking up and seeing my husband. The sad, faraway look in his eyes was not the look of a happy father.

I said, "What's wrong?"

He sat down and said, "I have some bad news."

I asked, "Is she alive?"

He said, "Yes."

I asked, "Is her heart ok?"

He said, "Yes."

I asked, "What is wrong?"

He said, "She has Down syndrome."

I asked, "Is that all?" I was so relieved! I knew I could love her and make her life the best it could be. That day they let me hold her. She was absolutely perfect in my eyes. She was a little angel from Heaven.

They told us she would probably be in the hospital for six weeks until she gained some weight. Not our girl, she went home in six days; she has always loved to eat. I had not only joined the Mommy Club, but now I had joined a new club which I did not yet understand. I was now forever linked to the special needs community wherever I would go.

When Chelsea was first born I was given the story "Welcome to Holland" by Emily Perl Kingsley. I absolutely love this story. The author talks about how people think they are headed to Italy. All their plans were to go to Italy, but instead their plane lands in Holland. The people say, "Oh no, I was supposed to go to Italy. Everyone else is going to Italy."

As I read it, I realized that I, too, now lived in Holland, and like the story says, it truly takes a while to get over the loss of all your plans and dreams. But one day you wake up and you begin looking around Holland and you see beautiful flowers and other lovely scenery. The sites, the sounds, and the people you meet are different than you dreamed or expected, but you come to appreciate it and begin to see Holland as a special place, and a special gift.

Like the people who did not land in Italy, my early thoughts of loss were, "My little girl will never drive; she will never go to college; she may never get married. Would she ever get to go to prom?" Then after adjusting to life in Holland, my thoughts changed and became, "Thank You, Lord, we only have one high school student learning to drive!"

But this girl most certainly will go to college and she has her first job working in a pre-school. She is making plans to go to a special needs prom next year. As for getting married, she has names for all of her future kids and she tells me, "Don't worry, Mom, when I get married we will live next door and always come home for dinner. Oh never mind, let's just all get a big, huge house with a pool and water slide and we will all live together forever!"

That sounds like Heaven doesn't it?

God brought another friend my way that would change our lives forever. Her name is Jane and she is a special needs teacher who helped direct the volunteers for the "Joni and Friends Family Camp" in Southern California each year. One day Jane called our church and set up a lunch appointment with my husband. I don't think she even knew we had a special needs baby. Ed asked me to come to the lunch, and I brought our little baby girl along. Jane saw our little Chelsea and asked to hold her. I could see the love she had for children with special needs; it forged an immediate bond between us. God had divinely appointed this luncheon. Through Jane we would start an amazing Special Needs program at our church, and through Jane's invitation we would be forever changed through the Joni and Friends Family Camp.

Our world and ministry, our borders and boundaries, and our heart for families with special needs became so much bigger from that day on.

Do you know that over eighty percent of couples that are touched by special needs in their family divorce? Not only is that statistic staggering, but many families with special needs attend no church at all. We heard story after story from families that had been told they were not welcome in a church because the church could not meet their needs. Most churches never even tried! It was heartbreaking to hear, and I knew from that day on I wanted to make a difference in the lives of those touched by disabilities.

I can understand the strain that is put on so many marriages. The initial news is a shock that no one expects and there are no answers to all of the inevitable questions. When Chelsea was born, my husband, Ed, had a really hard time. He researched vitamins and everything known to man trying to fix things for her. What can I say? It's a "man" thing.

That man couldn't fix her, but she has certainly fixed him. When he's cranky, she'll say, "Now, Handsome, are we a little cranky today? I think you just need some gelato." She has him wrapped around her little pinky, and she's certainly stolen his heart.

Our church and home have been wonderful safe places for Chelsea, but public school has been tough on her, at times. Referring to her school, she would often say to me, "I'm different here." One memory I will never get over is going to visit Chelsea in kindergarten. While we were sitting out on the patio enjoying a snack together, all the other kids at her table got up and left. I overheard them saying, "Don't sit by her." It made me very sad. I was wiping away my tears, subtly, I thought, when I felt Chelsea reach over and pat my arm. She said, "Don't worry, Mom. You're my best friend."

Having a child with special needs brings new compassion for weaknesses, and new awareness of strengths into your life. There are challenges at home, church, school, and in the community. It's all uncharted waters.

Chelsea's always the embodiment of innocence, compassion, and true unconditional love. One day she came home and was trying to tell me about a boy in her class. I kept saying, "His name is Caesar?"

She said, "No, Mom."

She was getting a little frustrated with me because I just couldn't get what she was trying to tell me. Finally, I just said, "I'm sorry, Chelsea, you will have to show me what you are talking about."

She went on to tell me, "The black boots came."

I asked more questions, "Whose black boots?"

"The men in blue wore them," she told me. Finally she just started shaking her arms and legs and head.

"Oh!" I said, "Seizure? The little boy in your class had a seizure?"

She shook her head yes. The little boy in her class had died and she was very sad.

She went back to school the next day and sang a song to all the kids to tell them Jesus loved each of them so much that he personally carried the little boy home to heaven. Her teacher told me it was like watching an episode from "Touched by an Angel"!

Our special girl has her own personal style. She sings at the top of her lungs using her own keys and pitch. She always wears two different socks that do not match. This is her signature look and she's good with it. I constantly buy her new packs of socks, but she just mixes them up to her liking.

My angel loves to go on cruises, too. Her two favorite things are the food and the water slides. Chelsea is actually a food connoisseur and she loves room service. I can hear her little voice saying, "Oh yeah!" In fact, Chelsea lives her entire life with a room service mentality. She never worries about the big stuff or the small stuff. She simply knows that her Heavenly Father will provide her with everything she needs. She is the first to make the call and get up and go to the door to let Him in. Chelsea has taught me a lot about room service. With God, help is available 24/7. God delights in the prayers of His children. All we need to do is call Him and open the door to let Him bring the nourishment and comfort we need.

Chelsea repeatedly surprises me with her discernment – usually at the most relevant and pertinent moments. She is like a wise old soul in a young lady's body. She senses the needs and hurts of others and yet she never has a bad word to say about anyone. The strongest comment she will make is, "Not good!" One time she was telling me something very insightful and I was trying to figure out how she would know that and why she was telling me. She merely said, "I have my Father's eyes." Astonishing! She's said this to me on more than one occasion and each time I've listened, marveled, believed and obeyed.

I have come such a long way since that initial landing in Holland. I see more beauty than I've ever seen in my life. This little girl loves all of us with an unconditional love that is beyond comprehension. She is a light that shines brightly for God wherever she goes.

Do you know that if the doctors had known her diagnosis through amniocentesis before her birth, they would have encouraged me to choose abortion? The world's logic is unfathomable to me. I cannot begin to tell you all I would have missed, but I would certainly have missed out on life, and the very essence of love, itself.

In the Bible, Hebrews 13:2 says we are to reach out and give hospitality to strangers. This scripture warns us that there are people who have entertained angels without even knowing it. They totally missed it! I don't want to miss God's visitation for even one moment. I am fully aware that Chelsea is the closest thing to an angel I have ever known, but she is the one doing the entertaining.

Someone once told me that God places special needs kids in the homes of special parents who will love them, but I believe the opposite is true for us. God put this little angel, Chelsea, in our home to bless us with unconditional love and joy beyond measure.

Joy abounds wherever Chelsea is. She knows the words to every song and sings with all her might. She is a dancer at heart and loves nothing more than praising God. Each Sunday as we are practicing for worship, I look up and see Chelsea when she arrives, dancing down the aisle to her spot on the front row. When she shows up, she definitely brings her all for God.

I have discovered that those with special needs bring an extraordinary love, strength, and sense of the presence and nearness of God. I Corinthians 1:27b (NIV) tells us, "God chose the weak things of the world to shame the strong." This little girl has a closeness to God that transcends all barriers, walls, and the hardest of hearts. Her strength in weakness is truly humbling. I do not understand how Chelsea can discern such depth of insight. How she perceives a lot of what she says, I don't know. But this one thing I do know - this little girl truly has her Father's eyes.

Baggage Claim

"I have not achieved it, but I focus on this one thing: Forgetting the past and looking forward to what lies ahead. I press on to reach the end of the race and receive the heavenly prize for which God, through Christ Jesus is calling us."—Phil. 3:13-14 (NLT)

Denise & Debbie cruising

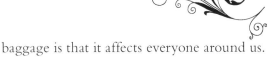

The problem with baggage is that it affects everyone around us.
The more baggage we carry with us, the slower it goes.
It is possible for us to miss our next cruise
if we get stuck down in the baggage basement of our lives.

The secret to any cruise is in the Baggage Claim!

Funny Denise ...

I am disorganized. I was born this way. I have a multitude of friends who have tried their best to organize me and my life and they all failed miserably. I know the general vicinity of where something is, for instance, a shirt I need is somewhere in the house. A document is somewhere in my office. In the general vicinity is about as organized as I get.

It's a fact of life that I will always be a last-minute kind of girl. Planning is not one of my strong suits. I would love to be one of those people who pack for vacations ahead of time. You have seen them, you know who they are; you may actually be one of them. You recognize them at the airport or on a cruise ship. They are the ones with the matching luggage, purse, and shoes, which also match a bow in their hair. They get to the front of the line with everything out of their purse, paper-clipped together and folded neatly in the correct order. They are dressed to the nines with no hair out of place. They purchased their magazines in advance of their trip so they didn't have to pay five times what they are worth at the airport, and they probably brought along a healthy snack to enjoy on the plane. It's always on my mind. I know I should do it early to avoid forgetting anything, but it never seems to happen that way. Except this one time ...

My son stayed with my folks during the summers from the time he was ten until he was seventeen. He loved going on vacation with them and it gave my husband and me some quality time together. This particular summer I was to fly to San Antonio, spend four days visiting with my folks, then return home with my son. I decided to be organized; I started to pack two days before I was leaving. The morning I was to leave, I finished my bathroom routine and packed each and every last-minute item in the suitcase, zipped it up, and set it by the bedroom door for my husband to load in the car. The airport was two hours away so we left in plenty of time. We talked all the way to San Diego and had a lovely lunch. We made it to the airport just in time for me to check my luggage, get through the checkpoint and board the plane.

My husband is a man of few words whenever I am leaving town, so he does the "Texas boot and drive." He pulls up to the curb, opens the trunk, takes out the luggage, quick kiss and off he goes. This time was no different, except for the look on his face as he opened the trunk. As I waited on the curb for him to bring my luggage around and get my second kiss goodbye I heard the words you don't want to hear when getting ready to board a plane to go on vacation.

"Babe, where's your luggage?"

"What do you mean where's my luggage?"

"I mean, where is your luggage?" he said.

I said, "Did you look everywhere in the trunk?"

He said, "It's a Jeep Wrangler; the trunk is like one foot by two foot!"

I said, "Well, look again. It has to be there. I packed it; you loaded it, where is it?"

He said, "You loaded it, I didn't."

In twenty-five years of marriage, I have never loaded a piece of luggage; and yet somewhere in my husband's brain he decided this would be the one time I loaded my own luggage. I couldn't move; I just stood there staring at the one foot by two foot trunk of the jeep in disbelief. A baggage handler approached me and asked if I needed help with my luggage.

I said, "Yes, I do!"

He approached the Jeep and looked in, he looked at me, he looked at my husband, and we all three looked back at the Jeep.

He said, "Ma'am, do you have any luggage?"

I looked at my husband and shot mental-darts at him. In the meantime, airport security approached and asked if there was a problem. Again I looked at my husband and daggers shot out of my eyes.

The baggage handler said, "We're looking for her luggage."

Airport Security said, "Where is her luggage?"

My husband said, "It should be in the trunk but my wife forgot to …" and then silence.

There was no kiss goodbye that day, but neither did I miss my plane due to baggage check-in. And, yes, my husband did survive. In fact, they say he may actually be able to walk again someday (just kidding!)

When I arrived in San Antonio, I was the last one to get off the plane. I sat there pondering what lie I was going to use to explain the luggage mishap. I mean, I couldn't admit I didn't load my own luggage.

My mom's last words before I left the house were, "Do you have everything?"

I felt like a child when she asked that question, so to prove how truly mature I was, I answered sarcastically, "No Mom! I left my head at the house." Truth was, I sort of did.

I rode the escalator down to the lower level to meet my folks and my son. After all the hugs, we slowly walked to the baggage area to claim my absentee luggage. We watched all the luggage come down the chute. I waited with anticipation, hoping that maybe, just maybe my luggage somehow mysteriously had arrived at the airport in San Antonio and would come flying out of that chute at any moment. Soon all the luggage was taken and I was left standing there with a look of disbelief on my face. I knew my parents would have sympathy for me and run me over to Wal-Mart to get undies, shirts and shorts and they wouldn't be the wiser.

My father turned to my mother and said, "I bet she forgot to bring her luggage!"

My mother said, "No…not Denny! I asked her if she forgot anything and she assured me she had everything, except her head!"

I said, "Well, maybe it got lost and is on its way to Pittsburgh."

Both parents in unison responded with, "Your husband called and it's lost alright, in your bedroom."

It's been many years since that episode but I assure you that no matter where I'm headed, my mother will specifically call me when I am in the car and ask me if I remembered to not only pack my luggage but did I also bring it?

A few years later on a cruise ship, I got my payback. It was the last night of the cruise and my parents were in the room next to mine. I had laid out all of my clothing for the next day's departure, kept a small bag for my bathroom items and nightgown, and placed the remaining luggage in the hallway. My parents had cruised before so I felt sure they knew about the ritual of placing your luggage in the hallway the night before. They remembered that part, just not the part about keeping clothes with you to wear the next morning when disembarking.

The next morning I arrived at breakfast and noticed my mom sitting alone. I asked where my father was and she just chuckled.

I said, "Really, Mom, where's Daddy?"

She said, "I couldn't bring myself to walk with him to breakfast so I left early from the stateroom. He should be along soon." Then she chuckled a little more.

Then I saw him, walking with his arms to his side and a jacket on. He kept tugging at the jacket as he walked and I noticed some hair coming out of the top. This was unusual for my daddy as he normally wears a collared shirt. Then I realized what the issue was. Daddy had forgotten to lay out clothes the night before.

My father ate his breakfast like he had duct tape wrapped around his arms and body. He barely moved for fear his stomach would be exposed for all to see.

As we left the ship that day, I had to chuckle as I watched a cute little couple in front of me disembarking. The man in front of me was pulling the front of his jacket down with each step, and the lady behind him was pulling the back of the jacket down at the same time; what a funny pair they were.

Yep, that's my precious mom and daddy.

Just Debbie …

Without our baggage we feel naked. Not just in the physical sense, but also mentally. So much of the time our baggage defines who we are, but it shouldn't. How many times are you defined as the divorcée, the spouse of an alcoholic, the mother of an addict, the woman with cancer? To be truthful, we all have baggage, don't we?

In reality, we all have things we need to deal with in the Baggage Claim area. Some of us have forgotten where we put our baggage; some of us are pretending we don't have any. But in reality, we all need to pay a little more attention to this area of our life, as it can make or break us.

My most unforgettable memory from any cruise also involves baggage. It's hard to believe how such a small, obscure bag could have such a big impact on our cruise, our life, and our soul. Nevertheless, when I think of the word "cruise" I think of baggage.

Of course, I remember lobster dinners, chocolate soufflés, comedy shows, beautiful scenery, walks around the deck, midnight dessert buffets, but the funniest memory of all involves luggage, or the lack of it.

My first cruise was with my husband before we had children. We went with my parents on a Christian cruise that set sail out of Florida. The cruise was an absolute blast. We had so much fun seeing all of our friends, going to concerts, and Bible studies; it was "good to the last drop" just like the old coffee commercial put it. The last drop for us came with an early Sunday morning phone call right before we were to disembark and catch our flight home.

My mother is a very early riser; come rain or shine, she is up at the crack of dawn. We were sound asleep in our tiny stateroom when our phone rang; my dad was calling. Now, my dad is not the type of person to make an early phone call so I knew something was up. He sounded nervous, extremely nervous.

If you've ever been on a cruise, you know to set your luggage out in the hallway the night before you depart, and you simply keep your overnight bag. They come by and take away your bulky luggage so you don't have to carry it off the ship yourself. This wonderful service adds to the feeling of pampered luxury for the passengers and, I am sure, saves the walls of the ship from being scuffed and scarred by passengers hurrying down the hallways laden with heavy bags. The ship's crew has this procedure down to a discipline so precise it could be rocket science. I might add that my father was a pastor, not a rocket scientist.

My mother's nickname in those days was "Pinky." She got the nickname when I was in college and my parents went along as chaperones on a trip. My mom had a pink nightgown, with a matching robe and slippers. My buddies, who were also college students, had never seen anyone in their entire lives this well-coordinated at bedtime. They just didn't know my mom. The nickname stuck, and so did her ensemble. Mama Pinky was up even earlier than usual as she wanted to get ready to meet everyone for breakfast before departure and didn't want to be rushed.

She began looking around for her clothes. She looked high and low. Her stateroom was about the size of a matchbox, so it didn't take much time. She had no clothes! She had absolutely nothing. There was no jacket, pants, or shirt. She was simply pretty in pink.

This was a very early Sunday morning and every shop on the ship was closed as we were docked and ready to depart. My poor dad sounded like a man who was awaiting a death sentence at trial, but there would be no bond for him nor was there a lawyer. He needed all the help he could get as he was the person who had, for some insane reason, packed her clothes away and set the suitcases out in the hallway to be whisked away by the luggage fairies. None of us could begin to fathom what he had been thinking. The poor man was a wreck; thus, the early morning 9-1-1 phone-call from my dad to our stateroom.

Unfortunately, our luggage had also been removed. All we had were the clothes on our backs. We hurried to their room to find my mother dressed in pink, including her pink slippers. She was pretty in pink from head to toe. Not happy, but pretty.

I was thinking to myself, "This could be much worse. Some people don't wear anything to sleep in. At least she looks nice."

She was not the least bit encouraged by this line of thinking. She was pacing, and it was a very small room. Either we find her clothes or she was not getting off the boat.

I was thinking, "That works for me! We can just stay onboard and go for another week of cruising. This could be a good thing."

She found no humor in the moment. We were now on a mission to find the Holy Grail, I mean, holy girdle. We needed an entire outfit, and we needed it quickly.

Did you know there is an entire other world on a cruise ship? This vast land is hidden down under, in the lowest recesses of the ship's belly, filled with rows and rows of luggage as far as the eye can see. It was reminiscent of the last scene in "Raiders of the Lost Ark" only we weren't searching for the Ark of the Covenant. It was not very cool down there, either. We searched from aft to stern, from top to bottom, from side to side. Our entire focus and goal in life had become baggage. All we cared about was baggage. We could not get off of this ship without baggage. We had become Baggage Claim specialists. The entire bottom of the ship was filled with baggage, baggage, baggage. It was not glamorous, festive, or filled with life and happiness. It was just bags filled with stuff.

Whenever we think of that cruise we laugh. We all still laugh today whenever we remember one word: baggage.

I was actually stunned by what I learned. I could have gone on cruise after cruise and never given baggage a second thought. Yet, it is an extremely essential part of each and every cruise. It needs proper handling and requires major planning. Without that early morning phone call, I would have lived the rest of my life blissfully unaware of the full impact of baggage.

Not only can we choose our cruise, but we have something to say about our own personal baggage claim. No matter what trip we find ourselves on, baggage has its part. My mom was trapped inside her little stateroom because that one seemingly insignificant thing was missing and it controlled her life on that particular day. In much the same way, our baggage can lock us in place and control our lives, but sometimes the effects can last a lifetime.

There is an often overlooked story in the Bible. We have all heard of Abraham as he was a very important person in the lineage of the Jewish people. Abraham was considered a friend of God, but can you remember his father's name? Have you ever heard of him?

Abraham's father was Terah. Genesis 11:27 tells us a little bit about Terah's life. He not only had Abram (later renamed Abraham) but he also had a son named, Haran. Haran died in Ur of the Chaldeans, in the land of his birth.

In the next verse we see that God is at work in the life of Abraham. God is leading him to the Promised Land. It tells us that when they came to the place called Haran, they settled there. Terah (Abraham's father) lived two hundred and five years, and he died in Haran - the town with the very same name as his son. Terah never made it to the Promised Land. He arrived in the city of Haran, and stayed there. Was it too hard, too painful, and too demanding to move on? He lived the rest of his life in the land of sorrow and loss, stopping short of God's goal. Our baggage has a way of affecting others around us, including our own families.

In Genesis 12 we see God tell Abraham to move on, leave his father's house, and follow God's leading to the Promised Land. This decision had to be incredibly difficult for Abraham. He had to leave his earthly father in the pain of his past to follow God's leading for his future. Do you know that after Abraham moved on, the Bible says nothing more about Terah? As far as we know, his life story ends in Haran, the land of his pain and loss.

The problem with baggage is it affects everyone around us. The more baggage we carry, the slower it goes. It's possible for us to miss our next cruise if we get stuck in the baggage basement of our lives. Abraham had a great calling on his life and Terah could have been there to see it, but he was never heard of again. That is some powerful food for thought.

I've often wondered what my life would be like today if it were not for a friend who helped me unpack my bags. I went off to college, but I really didn't want to be there. In fact, my bags stayed packed the whole first month I was there. Not a dresser drawer was filled with my clothes. Not a picture was hung on my bulletin board. I had not truly committed to going on that cruise. God, however, knew my every need and He had gone before me. As Jeremiah 29:11-13 says, "He had a plan for good in my life" even before I could see it. This plan started with unpacking my bags.

The summer after high school graduation, I went on a youth mission trip to an orphanage. Our choir was touring and I played the piano, sharing a piano bench with another pianist. When I got to Bible College that fall, one of the first people I met was that girl. We had shared a bench. She had turned my pages when I played, and I had turned her pages when she played for her group. We were now music majors in the same school, on the same floor, in the same dorm.

One day she came by my room to take me to some event and she asked me why I hadn't hung any pictures. I said, "I don't know if I want to stay." She realized that all my bags were still packed, just sitting there.

She looked at me and said, "Which drawer do you want your underwear in?"

And that is pretty much how we met and became best friends.

What I can tell you for a fact is this: I would not be the person I am today without the friends that God has sent my way. I would most certainly not be in ministry, either.

What would my life have been like if I had never unpacked my bags?

We all face tipping points. These are the moments that our scale can tip one way or another. We either unpack our bags and move forward or stay right where we are and stagnate. Abraham's father, Terah, just wanted to stay put. He was so sad about losing his son that he stayed in the land that bore his son's name. He was more concerned about the dead than the living. He could have gone on with his living son and reached the Promised Land, but he stayed in the land of his grief. If we truly want to experience God, we must be willing to choose the cruise, get on the boat, and claim our baggage.

Perhaps you're saying to yourself, "I want to get in the boat with Jesus. I want to see Him work in my life, but I don't know which boat to take. I don't know where I'm going or what I'm supposed to do." Maybe you're in a spot similar to the one I was in when it was time for me to unpack my bags but I had no clear direction or desire to go anywhere. I get that, I really do.

I never set out to go to college, be a pastor's wife, choose adoption, or have a special needs child. This was all part of the cruise that God had in mind for me. I'm eternally blessed by His sovereign plan for my life. I can see the faces of all the people He has allowed me to touch along the way; people that were reached because of the avenues He selected for my life.

Not only that, but I didn't plan or intend to write this book you are reading today. I had no plans - none, nada. One day, as we were riding in the car coming back from celebrating my birthday by floating on a lazy river, Denise asked me if I would write with her. We had never even discussed writing before. I knew she was as funny as all get out, but I had just learned for myself that she could write, as well.

She claims there was a long pause when she asked me if I would co-author this book, but there was no long pause for me. I thought about the question and knew I had been destined to write. I felt an amazing peace because I know the source of my passion and love for writing. I just looked at her and said, "Yes, I would." It was a done deal!

Since I uttered those words and got on the boat there has not been a day that the words have not poured into my soul and out of me like cool springs of water in the hot desert. (OK, I live in the desert and it has been, like, a hundred and twenty degrees here.)

In less than a year's time we have written three books, and God is filling me with ideas for more. I have absolutely no idea where these books are going, how we will pay for them or what in the world God wants to do with them. I do know this, I do not want to be like Terah who sat in Haran missing out on life while mourning what once was. I want to choose the cruise, get on the boat, and unpack my baggage. Whatever happens to me along the way will just help get me where God wants me to be. Every up or down is another story to write. I see the humor, am filled with hope, and since I have unpacked those bags of mine, I am blessed with God's healing and direction.

Never forget to take the important things in life with you. Remember to hold tightly to the essential things you'll need to get through life (like your clothes for that day).

Change is hard. It just is. We want to hold on to the old, but if we hold on too long, we might miss what God has planned for our future. The only way to embrace God's plan is to let go of your old stuff and hang in there to see what He has planned.

I'm thankful for lost baggage that was found and reclaimed, and for old luggage that was unpacked. Most of all, I'm thankful for those special people along the way that love us and help us leave the old and move into the new so that we can embrace the life that God has called us to live.

The secret to any good cruise truly is in the baggage claim!

Call Me Crazy...

"Without faith it is impossible to please God."—Heb.11:6a (NIV)

Crazy Denise at VBS

We are inviting you to get on the boat and hang on tight
because we are going for the ride of our lives. It will be
our finest hour and at the end, God will say, "By faith…"
and then He will say your name and ours with a smile.
In that moment it will all have been worth the ride.

What floats your boat?

Funny Denise …

There are days when I wake up in the morning and think to myself how much fun it would be to just act crazier than a loon that day. I saw a post on Facebook that said, "Today when a stranger approaches and speaks to me I am going to slowly turn to them and softly whisper, 'You can see me?'" I sometimes think it would be easier to just play "Nutso" and hope the world takes pity and lets me be me.

It seems like only yesterday when I was twenty-something and I could run, and jump, and just enjoy life. Today, I woke up a fifty year old, and if I run and jump, I will have to grease up with Ben-Gay and change my drawers! How is it that our minds make us feel like a twenty year old, and yet when we look in the mirror, we see our mother's body?

Every year I lead the goofy part of Vacation Bible School (VBS); the part that everybody wants to watch and yet no adult wants to lead. It's the part where you end up with a pie in the face, water over your head, props exploding, walls tumbling, and the most ridiculous outfits ever conceived. I have been a nutty professor with a clothes hanger weaved into my hair to resemble Pippy Long stocking, a deep sea diver with snorkel, fins and wetsuit, a redneck fisherman with bib overalls, a pirate with cape, sword and boots, but this year takes the cake! Debbie decided I needed to dress as a Squirrel. Not your average squirrel, but one with multi-colored striped socks with individual toes, a red cape, a "Captain America" shirt, a chipmunk cap with an A on it, long red gloves, a red and white boa, and a rat nose. Not only did I not resemble a cute little squirrel, I actually scared a few of the little kids, and my mother!

I have to say that sometimes Nutso isn't such a bad thing. Since I spend the rest of my year working as an accountant, going Nutso for a week is pretty cool. This year we planned to do an encore of one of our Nutso skits for church on Sunday. I decided this was my last hurrah for the year so I was going out with a bang. In my mind, I saw myself running down the aisle of the sanctuary leaping in the air and yelling, "Woo Hoo! Woo Hoo! I got it! I got it!"

In my mind it looked fabulous - totally hilarious - and the crowd would go wild. I couldn't wait for my cue. It was my turn, and off I ran. Nadia Comaneci had nothing on me! I was going to run and leap in the air like it was the Olympics all over again. I took off running and in my mind I was a super hero with my red cape flying behind me. I was twenty again and I would prove it!

I got to the end of the long aisle and jumped least six feet in the air (more like six inches) and yelled, "Woo-Hoo!! Woo-Hoo!!" It was a spectacular leap! It would have gotten tens from all the judges, but the landing was something completely unanticipated. I came down on my ankle and thought I would pass out. The audience thought it was part of the act as I was hobbling up the stairs to the stage. I looked at my acting partner who thought it was just me being crazy and went along with it. Little did they know the pain that was radiating from my ankle to my knee. I finished my lines with much less enthusiasm than I had started and was supposed to fly out of the sanctuary. Let's just say I was the crippled flying squirrel at best.

Just Debbie …

Do you remember hearing some crazy stories at VBS as a kid growing up? Things like:

- A man is swallowed by a whale and actually lives inside it for three days before it throws him up onto dry land.
- A young boy kills a giant with just a slingshot.
- A huge sea is parted in the middle and a group of people walk across to the other side on dry land.
- A man is buried in a tomb for three days and when he hears his name he comes walking out of the tomb, good as new.
- God made the entire world in just six days, and then took a break and rested on the seventh day.
- This defies all logic. This is crazy talk.

When I was a kid, one of my favorite VBS songs was pretty crazy, as well. There were a million verses to this endless song, so I will just give you a summary of the highlights. If you grew up singing this song you will probably not be able to get it out of your mind for the rest of the day, but go ahead and sing along. It's catchy, very catchy.

The Lord said to Noah,

There's gonna be a floody, floody,

Get those children out of the muddy, muddy,

Children of the Lord.

This little kid's song reminded us that it rained for forty daysie daysies, and that it almost drove those animals crazy, crazy! Now, I would say that the animals were not the only crazy ones in this story. A man named Noah is the one who built this Arky Arky out of gopher barky barky.

For one hundred years he and his sons faithfully worked on building a boat. He constructed it miles away from any body of water. The people had probably never seen or smelled rain. Genesis 2:5-6 leads many to believe that Noah had never seen rain either. We do know with all certainty that they had never encountered a flood. So the people mocked them for one hundred years.

After a hundred years of construction they got on the Ark and simply sat there in the dry, barren land for seven days - seven long days. Nothing happened … nothing!

Then the floodgates opened. The waters flooded the earth for forty days and forty nights. This was no mere rainstorm. This was beyond crazy. Water came up from the bottom of the earth, and water came down from the heavens. Everything on the earth was destroyed. All that remained were eight righteous people, seven of each clean animal, and two of every unclean animal, male and female.

Noah was five hundred years young when he had his sons. He was six hundred years young when they got on the ark, and the Bible tells us that he was six hundred and one years old when he got off of that stinky boat (Genesis 8:13). I would guess more than the animals were crazy, crazy by then.

This was the first cruise ever recorded in the history of mankind and it was a doozy. Everything living on the earth was destroyed; only Noah and his family were saved. This is beyond comprehension. Why had it happened? How does any of it make sense?

Hebrews 11:7 (NLT) offers us this commentary on Noah, "It was by faith, that Noah built a large boat to save his family from the flood. He obeyed God who warned him about things that had never happened before." The first thing we need to understand about God is found in His warning.

Imagine the cost of this faith for Noah. For one hundred years he labored to build a boat, and for one hundred years he lived a sermon through his obedience by building an ark exactly as God instructed. A warning resounded to the people ... *repent!* Each day Noah's building project was the biggest news around. Did anyone repent, help them, or join them? They did not!

The Bible tells us that Noah was righteous, blameless, and he walked with God. (Genesis 6:9) We are told, "Noah did everything just as God commanded him." --Genesis 6:22 (NIV)

Of the day and age in which Noah lived, the Bible says, "The Lord saw how great the wickedness of the human race had become, and that every inclination of the thoughts of the human heart was only evil all the time. The Lord regretted that he had made human beings on the earth, and his heart was deeply troubled." --Genesis 6:5-6 (NIV)

There was nothing in the world worth saving except Noah, his little family, and the animals that God had made. The scriptures tell us that Noah revered God, so he took Him at His word. What God said He would do, Abraham believed to be true. There was no water, no river nearby; no proof as far as the eye could see that there could ever be such a thing as a flood. There was only one thing afloat on this day, Noah's faith.

Not only did God provide a warning, but He also provided a way through.

We need to take note that even though Noah was righteous, blameless, and obedient, he was not delivered from his troubles.

How many times have we asked God, "Why me?"

"Why are you letting this happen to me?"

"What have I done wrong?"

Perhaps - just perhaps - we have done something *right*.

Noah lived among a people that were wicked in thought, intent, and actions. The earth was completely filled with violence. Yet, they all seemed to be getting by with it. They were mocking Noah, but nothing was fazing them at all. This kind of sounds like our world today, doesn't it?

Luke 17:26-27 (NIV) tells us the rest of the story. "Just as it was in the days of Noah, so also will it be in the days of the Son of Man. People were eating, drinking, marrying and being given in marriage up to the day Noah entered the ark. Then the flood came and destroyed them all."

God did not deliver Noah *from* the trouble. He delivered him *through* it.

Hebrews 11:7 says it all, "By faith, Noah ..." Notice that Noah did exactly what God instructed him to do. He did his part, and God did all the rest!

Let me ask you a question: How does one gather up two of every animal known to man? How long would it take to find every ant, spider, skunk, and hippo? This is a physical impossibility for man. The God who made each animal, simply called them by name.

How many times do we sit and worry about things that are impossible for us, and refuse to obey the task God has given us to do?

Genesis 8 begins with these words, "But God remembered Noah ..." Sometimes when we are going through trials we feel abandoned by God. We have difficulty understanding why God is letting us go through a hard time.

God did not let Noah and his family escape the great flood, but He did take them safely through it. God always warns His people and He provides a way through the storm.

There is one more important part to this story. God also provides a way *out*.

I would love to end here with the VBS happy ending about how they landed on the dry land, but I would be remiss if I did not include the untold part of the story for you. The complete ending is so important for us to know.

Noah's three sons had children to repopulate the earth and everything was getting back to normal. Noah was the first man in the Bible to build an altar of remembrance to the Lord. The only problem with this altar of remembrance is that Noah forgot to remember.

Noah got comfortable, complacent…and drunk. Perhaps you are wondering what the problem is? After a cruise like that, who wouldn't need a little libation?

The Bible tells us that Noah "uncovered himself." You can look in the ninth chapter of Genesis to read more about this disappointing story. The Hebrew word used here means "shameful nakedness" and is associated with immoral behavior. It is different from the word that simply means to be naked.

Not only does the word used here tell us there was a problem, but we are told that there were consequences for what happened. Genesis 9:23 tells us that his youngest descendent which was apparently his grandson, Canaan, was cursed for his actions. Apparently, Canaan took advantage of his grandfather's drunken state and committed some immoral act with him.

His grandson had not been there to see God's mighty power during the flood. He had not seen his grandfather's amazing faith. Noah's faith had not been passed on in a way that would affect obedience in his grandson, and the result was that Noah cursed Canaan, his own grandson.

Noah didn't fall during his adversity but during his ease.

Noah obeyed God in his youth - alright he was a young six hundred! But after the adversity and in the latter days of his life, he let down his guard - big time. The Bible warns us to be careful. It is the times when we think we are standing strong that we most easily fall.

During our time together in this book we have shared many examples of our own personal struggles. There have been ordeals with waiting rooms, fears, sickness, infertility, adoption, special needs, cancer, and life-threatening moments.

God has always been there for His children and He always will be. He uses us to be the light for this dark world. That light shines especially bright when people watch us suffer and wait on God. We are the salt and light. God is preaching a warning to the world, not only through His Word, but through our actions and obedience. God often does not deliver us from trouble. While those in sin are partying around us, we are the ones facing trials. They are merely spectators watching our every move. While God does not deliver us from our suffering, He will provide a way through our troubles.

Noah's finest days were the days that he simply lived by faith doing everything God asked of him. His saddest days were when he let down his spiritual guard and lived by the flesh rather than walking by the Spirit. God's Word promises us that for every temptation, there is a way out.

So, what floats your boat? There is only one thing that will keep you afloat in the tough times when the floods come up and the rains come down. There is only one cruise that you can choose if you want to go with God. That cruise is *faith*.

James 1:2 tells us that we can still have joy even when we are facing trials because we know that the testing of our faith will bring perseverance. When that work is finished we will be complete and mature.

Perhaps you are wondering where the funny part is in this story. Where is the joy in these trials? Noah ended up missing the boat in his later life. You know, I cannot help but imagine how many funny stories there were when they were all on the boat for a whole year. Can you imagine all of the bodily functions, sights, smells, and noises that went on while they were locked up in there together? Even so, the joy was in the midst of the journey.

This book has been about Hope, Hilarity, and Healing for a woman's heart. I don't know about you, but I can tell you very clearly what I got out of this story. I want to be remembered for the cruise, not as a snoozer or a loser. Noah let down his guard and let his family down. His finest days were the days that his faith was afloat.

If you think about it, the man was crazy. He built a boat. He spent a hundred years completing a project. He spent only forty days in a flood, and one year waiting for the water to go down. His finest moments and his finest days were when he was simply crazy. There was no logic, no evidence, nothing but faith to guide him.

So here we are, two crazy ladies writing a book. There's no provision in sight, but there are plenty of people all around just watching. We have never written a book before and we don't know anything about gopher bark or how to build an ark. We are just putting this out there because God has put this message of hope inside our hearts. We can't rest until we build it. Somehow, if we build it, they will come. This worked in a baseball movie, but I wonder how many women watch those? Hmmm…all I can say is, the fact that you are reading this book right now means God sent us a boat and He alone kept us afloat.

"Our Faith Floats" was written because we don't want anyone to snooze and miss the cruise. We are inviting you to get on the boat and hang on tight because we are going for the ride of our lives. It will be our finest hour, and at the end, God will say, "By faith …" and then He will say your name and ours with a smile. In that moment, it will have been worth the ride.

Does anyone remember the chorus of the famous Arky song? I can still hear those words resounding in my ears as my favorite role model, Mama Martha, sang them each summer at church camp. "Rise and shine and give God the glory, glory ... Children of the Lord!"

By God's grace I want to keep that song going in my life because when all is said and done, I also want my kids to rise up and Call Me Crazy!

"If it seems we are crazy, it is to bring glory to God. And if we are in our right minds, it is for your benefit."
—2 Corinthians 5:13 (NLT)

"Just call us crazy"
—Denise & Debbie at VBS

Epilogue

Just Debbie . . .

Thank you for choosing to cruise with us through the pages of this book. Our desire was to share with you some of our life stories of high seas, high stress, and high winds. Yet, we are filled with high hope because we know who is in our boat and how the story is going to end. Right now things may not be the way we want them to be, but it will bring about the things God truly desires for each of us who is called according to His purpose and plan.

I gave one of these stories to a good friend to read and this was her response:

"Well...I smiled all the way through your manuscript; even the sadder parts. I thought about this for a while and realized my take on your story is different than someone who doesn't know your journey. I knew the

ending and it was all good. Better, actually than you ever expected. Then my light went on and I saw what God wanted me to see. We (Christians) know the ending and it's all good! No matter what life brings us, the trials, heartaches and pain, we can find HOPE in our future because we have God now. He will send us our lifelines and fellow journeyers (that a word?) to encourage us and walk with us until He returns. I'm so excited to read the finished product. I think God will touch many lives through your writing. I'll be waiting for more." J (Thank you, Linda!)

There is no promise from God that He will deliver us *from* trouble, but He will deliver us *through* it. Come hurricanes or high water - or a little of both - God is still there to calm the storms of our life with just His power, His presence, and His spoken word. We hope that the pages of this book have brought hope, hilarity, and healing to your heart.

"For I know the plans I have for you," declares the Lord,
"Plans to prosper you and not harm you,
plans to give you hope and a future.
Then you will call upon me and come and
pray to me, and I will listen to you.
You will seek me and find me when you seek me with
all your heart." —Jeremiah 29: 11-13 (NIV)

God loves Crazy Prayers

Do you know how patient God is with us when we pray? Over and over in the Bible we see that God heard the pleadings of His children and He came to rescue them from trouble. There is one very important qualification that enables us to hear God; that is *faith!*

What is faith and how can you have it today? We probably need to start with what faith is *not*. James 2:19-20 (NIV) tells us this, "You believe that there is one God. Good! Even the demons believe that--and shudder!" This passage goes on to tell us that faith without works is useless and dead!

Did you get that? Does it scare you like it scares me? We need to understand that even the demons believe in God. They do! They acknowledge Him and they shudder because of His power. The problem is that they *do not do anything* with that belief. There is no obedience, trust, or actions that follow their acknowledgment that God is real.

We do not show our faith in God by coming up with our own plans, dreams, and purposes and then asking God to bless our desires. Like Noah, we are called to respond to God's invitation to follow and obey Him in spite of the cost. The Bible tells us, "Without faith it is impossible to please God." (Hebrews 11:6a NIV) Real faith only comes through God's one and only son, Jesus Christ.

Many people would like to think that all roads of faith lead to Heaven, but listen to what God's Word says. Jesus answered,

"I am the way, and the truth, and the life. No one comes to the Father except through ME." (John 14:6 NIV)

Today you have a few choices to make. I can guarantee you that high seas and high stress will come your way. Will you choose the only cruise that will keep you afloat in spite of the high winds and waves? The only boat that will keep you afloat is FAITH in Jesus. He is the only life raft that God has provided. He is the only person that has overcome death, and the gift of His life has overcome the penalty of sin and death.

God loves crazy, sold out prayers that are spoken with heartfelt conviction. He will forgive your mess and give you a message of hope and faith just for the asking. Will you ask Him right now to be the Lord of your life?

You don't need to use fancy words. Just begin talking to God as you would a friend. Tell Him your fears and failures, and ask God to forgive you for your mistakes because He will do just that. Before you conclude your time in God's presence, ask Him to come into your heart and reign as the Lord of your life. This is your first step. Would you join me right now in a little prayer?

Dear God,

Thank you for the gift of your son Jesus Christ who died for my sins. I have made mistakes and I need your forgiveness and grace. I am truly sorry for wasted time, wrong choices, and for putting other things in place of You.

Forgive me, heal me, and lead me daily by the power of your Holy Spirit. I choose to leave my old life of fear and follow you all the rest of my days in faith.

Thank you for choosing to love me even when I am not worthy. I choose to receive your love and live the rest

*of my life in the light of that love. By your grace and
the gift of your Son's life on the cross I am now set free!
In Jesus' holy and powerful name I pray. Amen.*

Now find a friend, spend some time in fellowship with another Christian sister, and join the family of God by seeking out a great Bible teaching church. Romans 10:17 (NKJV) tells us that, "faith comes by hearing, and hearing by the Word of God." So you will need to spend time each day reading your Bible, praying and asking God what He desires for your life, and growing in fellowship in the body of Christ.

The Bible tells us about the early Christians and how they came to know Christ as their Lord and Savior. The apostle Peter was preaching about the good news of Jesus and they were convicted of their sins. So they asked him what they should do to be saved. Acts 2:38 (NKJV) tells us Peter's reply, "Each of you must repent of your sins and turn to God, and be baptized in the name of Jesus Christ for the forgiveness of your sins and the gift of the Holy Spirit.

Baptism is a lot like the ark that Noah built which saved him and his family from the destruction of the flood. It was not logical, common, or easily understood, yet God used it to rescue the people who were obedient. The ark was the symbol of God's faithfulness to His people, and of Noah's faith to follow God even when he could see no sign of water anywhere. He simply trusted and obeyed.

God is still seeking faithful people who will simply choose the cruise, and so our prayer today is that we will all be found faithful because we are willing to have a crazy, sold-out faith that is willing to obey God. High seas and high stress will come your way, but never forget who's in your boat. When God asks you to serve Him, take the gifts and passion He has placed inside you and set sail, because one day very soon we will meet Him face to face.

On that day your Heavenly Father will say, "By faith…" and He will speak your name and mine with a smile as He stretches out His hand to us because "Our Faith Floats!"

The Barefoot Authors

(Denise Rogers & Debbie Sempsrott)

The barefoot authors, Denise DeHaven Rogers & Debbie Strater Sempsrott have co-authored two other books: "Happy Dance" and "Tubular Therapy".

Each book cover shows feet without shoes. In Exodus 3:5b Moses encountered Almighty God and was told to take off his shoes, for the place where he was standing was holy ground. These images remind us that today this very same God still speaks, rescues, and provides. We call ourselves the barefoot authors because our shoes are off, and we stand in awe of a God that takes the ordinary and turns it into Holy Ground.

Debbie Sempsrott is a preacher's kid, pastor's wife, and the mother of two. As a mother she has joined the sisterhoods of special needs and adoptive moms. She serves in the area of worship and women's ministries. She is a graduate of Lincoln Christian

College and Hope International University with BA's in music and education. She also holds a Master's Degree in Marriage and Family Counseling.

Most of all she is best known as "Just Debbie". She is the girl next door that loves to play, laugh, and swim in any nearby pool. She is the Ethel who is writing with her best friend, Lucy. She is the other half of the wacky, wild sense of humor on each page. Debbie will break the mold on stereotypes for pastors' wives and put the awe in each and every story.

Denise is an accountant who co-owns her own bookkeeping business. Numbers roll through her mind from morning to night. However, she is not like any accountant you have ever met. She is as funny as the day is long. She has the red hair, antics, and facial expressions of Lucy, and, yes, most everyone loves her. Denise is the wife of a red-neck, mother of a firefighter, and the person everyone calls on to speak when they want things to be funny ... really funny. That is the only way she rolls! She is the queen of Spanx and the one we call "Funny Denise." After you read a bit, I think you will agree this girl is pure *cwazee*. She dares to say out loud what the rest of us secretly think.

The Barefoot authors' message is one of hope, hilarity, and healing. Each book contains grins and giggles, and tears and triumphs, for the seasons of a woman's soul. You will laugh, cry, and you will laugh until you cry.

It is our prayer that your cares will grow smaller, and your view of God will grow larger. When you lay each book down you will simply stand in awe of a God who meets each one of us privately, personally, and providentially. The God of Moses is alive, real, and still intervenes in our daily lives. He cares. He comforts. He comes near.

Together, our shoes will come off and we will stand in awe of a God that takes the ordinary and turns it into Holy Ground.

If you enjoyed **Our Faith Floats** we invite you to check out our other books at **WestBow Press** and at **Amazon.com**

"Happy Dance: Fabulous Through the Seasons" (Amazon.com)

This book is Grins & Giggles, Tears & Triumphs, and Hope and Healing for the Seasons of a Woman's Soul. We dare not wait for a perfect sunny day that we feel good enough. All of our tomorrows are based on the decisions we make today. If we are to be *Fabulous through the Seasons* we must take our Heavenly Father's hand, put our feet on His feet and simply learn to follow His lead. Let's celebrate! It's time to learn to Happy Dance.

"Happy Dance" has been given away to women's prisons, cancer centers, Hospice, The Ronald Mc Donald House, and to Chemo Angels. Contact us to see how you can help share "the dance" with hurting women.

"Tubular Therapy: Facing Fear with Friendship & Faith" (WestBow Press)

Do you remember your first childhood best friend? Can you recall simpler times of laughter, playing, and sharing when the cares of this life just seemed to melt away? Would you love to return to that feeling of safety, simplicity, and security?

Tubular Therapy is the story of one answered prayer, an unlikely friendship, and a surprising new ministry of two zany women writing with a fresh and hilarious new style. This story of friendship and faith is one crazy ride down life's lazy river. It is a grand adventure with ups and downs, hilarity and heartbreak, that will make you shake your head in disbelief. We dare to talk about what most keep hidden deep inside. "Tubular

Therapy" is LOL healing for the woman's soul. Have you gone tubular today?

(We invite you to write reviews for all
three books at Amazon.com.)

**Denise and Debbie are available to speak
for women's events and retreats.**

Visit our website at: www.ourfaithfloats.com.

You can contact us at: ourfaithfloats@yahoo.com.

Also like us at "Our Faith Floats" on Facebook.